PUBLI

## A Wild Australia Guide

# BUTTERFLIES
## & MOTHS

**PATRICK HONAN**

# Contents

**Left:** A newly-emerged Cruiser Butterfly
(*Vindula arsinoe*) hanging from the pupa.

# Introduction

Butterflies and moths together belong to the insect order Lepidoptera, the second-largest group of insects in the world (behind beetles). Lepidoptera is Greek for "scaly wings". Within the group there is a vast array of shapes, colours, lifestyles and sizes — ranging from 3 mm to more than 250 mm across the wings.

## IT'S ALL IN THE SCALES

Butterflies and moths are distinguished from other insects by the broad, overlapping scales covering their head, body and wings. Under the head they also usually have a coiled proboscis, which is used for feeding.

The scales on the body and wings are usually too small to be seen, but appear as a fine powder that rubs off when the wings are touched. Scales are extremely important because they help with the aerodynamics of the wings, can help moths escape from sticky spider webs and also give butterflies their spectacular colours.

## NIGHT-FLYING MOTHS & DAY-FLYING MOTHS

Moths and butterflies are extremely closely related and the differences between the two groups are very minor. The most primitive moths still have chewing mouthparts inherited from their ancestors. The coiled proboscis developed as other moths evolved and radiated into different families. Of the 145 or so families of the Lepidoptera today, butterflies make up only five. These five families arose from a single branch of moths, so butterflies may be seen simply as colourful, day-flying moths. The differences between butterflies and moths are often smaller than the differences between the various moth families. Consequently, there are no hard and fast rules that separate butterflies and moths. There are a few general guidelines, as outlined on the opposite page.

**Opposite, clockwise from top left:** The wings of butterflies and moths are covered with tiny scales that give them their colour and also aid in flight; Although many types of moths do not possess mouthparts and therefore cannot feed, all butterflies have a long proboscis for drinking nectar; Most moth species are small and inconspicuous, even when brightly coloured; Moths often conceal colourful hindwings with drab brown forewings; There are more than 20,000 moth and butterfly species in Australia, each with a distinctive type of caterpillar; Both butterflies and moths fly using both pairs of wings, which work together to act as a single pair of wings.

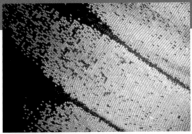 

 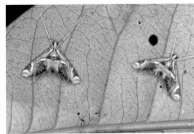

| Butterflies | Moths |
|---|---|
| • Generally fly during the day; | • Generally fly at night; |
| • Have brightly coloured wings; | • Usually have quite drab wings; |
| • Sit with their wings behind the body when at rest; | • Sit with their wings held to the sides or roof-like over their body when at rest; |
| • Have antennae that are smooth and end with a club at the tip; | • Have feathery antennae that do not have a club at the tip; |
| • Have wings that work together in flight due to a wide overlap between the forewings and hindwings. | • Have wings that work together in flight due to a "hook and bristle" system that locks together the forewings and hindwings. |

# The Cycle of Life

Like the great majority of insects, butterflies and moths have a four-stage life cycle. The first stage is the egg, which is usually laid by the female on or near the caterpillar's food plant. Some female moths, however, particularly ghost moths, scatter tens of thousands of eggs across the landscape as they fly overhead. Eggs come in an enormous range of shapes, sizes and colours and are often decorated with raised ridges or a series of ribs running from top to bottom. The eggs of most species usually hatch within a few days of being laid, but sometimes hatching may take several months, depending on the temperature and other environmental conditions.

## LIVING SAUSAGES

In the second stage of its life cycle, the caterpillar or larva is designed to consume enough food to build an adult moth or butterfly and usually to sustain it until death. The body is sausage-like, with a head that bears chewing mouthparts at one end and a series of legs underneath. The head capsule is hard and rounded, with tough mandibles. There are always three pairs of "true legs" under the head and usually a series of soft "prolegs" along the body, which are not true legs but outgrowths of the body. Each proleg usually ends with a flat plate that is lined with hooks for grasping branches. The sides of the body are lined with spiracles, which are used for breathing.

## THE GREAT TRANSITION

The pupa, or chrysalis, is a transitional stage between caterpillar and adult. In many moth species, the pupa is enclosed in a silken cocoon for protection. During pupation, the tissues of the caterpillar's body are broken down and an adult butterfly or moth is built in their place. The pupal stage does not feed and, in general, does not move. This is the most vulnerable stage of the life cycle and varies in length from several weeks to several years.

## THE FINAL STAGE

The adult stage, also known as the imago stage, is the most frequently seen stage of the life cycle. This stage lasts from several days to many months, during which the adults mate and the females lay eggs.

## LIFE CYCLE OF THE ORCHARD BUTTERFLY (*PAPILIO AEGEUS*)

**Above, clockwise from top left: 1.** Eggs laid on leaves of the food plant, a lemon tree;
**2.** A young caterpillar, this species mimics a bird dropping; **3.** An older caterpillar, now mottled
green for camouflage; **4.** The prepupa, a brief stage before the caterpillar pupates; **5.** The pupa,
once again camouflaged against the green background; **6.** An adult male; **7.** An adult female;
**8.** Adults mating.

# Growth & Metamorphosis

From hatching to pupation, caterpillars may increase up to 3000 times in weight. They feed on leaves, roots, stems, flowers, buds, fruit, lichen, moss, dead leaves, dead wood and fungi. Almost every species of plant on Earth is eaten by one species of caterpillar or another. Because of their constant feeding, caterpillars are a major influence on the structure of most plant communities. Some species of butterfly feed on only one species of plant, whereas others, such as the Cabbage White Butterfly (*Pieris rapae*), feed on more than 150 plant species.

## OUT WITH THE OLD

Because a caterpillar's skeleton is on the outside of its body instead of the inside, the caterpillar must shed this protective covering, called an exoskeleton, in order to grow. This is done by moulting. The caterpillar first takes air into its body to increase its size as much as possible, then the old skin splits down the back and the caterpillar extracts itself. The new skin usually requires several hours to dry before the insect is free to move off. Most species moult five times before pupating.

## THE MIRACLE OF METAMORPHOSIS

When it has finished feeding, the caterpillar finds a sheltered location, burrows underground, hangs from a stem of the food plant or sits upright attached by a silken girdle. It remains this way, as a prepupa, for a day or so before shedding its skin to reveal a pupa underneath. Many moth caterpillars spin a cocoon of silk just before pupation. Metamorphosis is a miraculous process whereby the entire caterpillar body is dissolved and replaced with the body of a moth or butterfly.

The adult usually emerges from the pupa in the early morning. The process only takes a couple of minutes, but the newly emerged butterfly must hang for several hours to allow its wings to dry before being able to fly away. If the adult becomes caught in the pupal skin or cocoon, or if it is unable to expand its wings properly, the wings will dry in the wrong shape and the adult will never be able to fly.

**Left:** When feeding or at rest, Chequered Swallowtails hold their wings high up behind the body.

**Top, left to right:** Butterflies do not construct a cocoon around the pupae but often support it with a silken girdle; Moth caterpillars emerging from their egg mass, which has been covered with the adult female's wing scales for protection; Moths usually pupate within a cocoon, which may be a simple silk structure or sometimes quite elaborate. **Centre, left to right:** A Common Eggfly caterpillar (*Hypolimnas bolina*) pupating. The process of pupation takes only one or two minutes, but the pupa requires several hours to harden properly. **Bottom, left to right:** A female Cruiser Butterfly (*Vindula arsinoe*) emerging from the pupa. Emergence takes only a couple of minutes but the wings require several hours to dry before the butterfly takes off.

# Reproduction

Before butterflies and moths can reproduce, males and females must first find each other. Female moths "call" to males by raising the abdomen when resting on a branch, sometimes exposing special "sex-scales" and releasing a sex-scent, or pheromone. Pheromones are a combination of organic chemicals; each species has a different combination, but they often share individual components. In some moth species, such as the Hercules Moth (*Coscinocera hercules*), the male uses his enlarged antennae to pick up the female's pheromones on the wind from more than a kilometre away.

## HILLTOP BATTLES

In many species of butterflies, the males are territorial and will patrol a particular patch of territory or perch in a prominent position to guard it. Males will briefly chase other species of butterflies, other flying animals such as birds and even humans that enter the territory. Common Eggfly males (*Hypolimnas bolina*) will "battle" with other males that enter their territory, flying around each other in spirals, which increase in altitude until one gives in and departs. Males of a large number of species set up territories on the tops of hills (a behaviour called "hilltopping") and females regularly visit to select a suitable partner. Courtship is rare in moths and attraction is based on pheromones.

## THE ART OF MATING AND EGG LAYING

Mating takes place with the male and female attached end to end, facing opposite directions. Sperm is passed from the male to the female, often in the form of a small packet. In some butterflies, such as the Clearwing Swallowtail (*Cressida cressida*), the male introduces a substance after mating that hardens into a plug, which prevents the females from mating again, at least for a time.

Eggs are laid on or around a food plant after the female has determined it is suitable food for the caterpillars. She usually does this using the chemicals produced by the plant as cues, sometimes scraping off the top layer of the leaf to access the chemicals underneath. Female Cruiser butterflies (*Vindula arsinoe*) do this with their front legs.

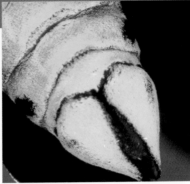

**Opposite:** Nymph butterflies mate end to end with their wings overlapping. If the male is unable to gain a footing he will hang with his legs folded up.
**Above, clockwise from top left:** Moths sometimes rest on leaves and expose the long scales at the end of the abdomen, releasing pheromones to attract mates; The tip of the abdomen of the male Cairns Birdwing Butterfly (*Ornithoptera priamus*) is covered with scales impregnated with powerful pheromones; The female Cairns Birdwing Butterfly will mate for many hours, carrying around the male, which is attached to the end of her abdomen.

# Wing Colour & Flight

Butterflies are renowned for their bright, brilliant colours, but moths less so. The natural colour of the insect exoskeleton is a dull brown, produced by the compounds that strengthen it. The wings of butterflies and moths are covered with millions of microscopic scales which, in the case of the Ulysses Butterfly (*Papilio ulysses*), reflect light off even tinier ridges and valleys. These structures produce a metallic sheen that changes as the light changes.

Some butterflies also have patterns that can only be seen in ultraviolet light. The plain wings of some butterflies, such as the Common Grass–yellow (*Eurema hecabe*), may have ultraviolet patterns that can be seen by other butterflies but not by humans.

## WHY SO COLOURFUL?

The colours of butterfly wings are not there for our pleasure. Some species are poisonous and advertise this to predators with contrasting red, yellow and orange with black. Others sport dark colours to absorb heat, or bright colours that reflect heat and keep the butterfly cool. Others, such as Lurchers (*Yoma sabina*), have bright and dark bands on the wings that break up the outline of the butterfly when basking in the sun.

## THE MIRACLE OF THE WING

The wings of most butterflies and moths are designed for sustained flight, sometimes for many months over many thousands of kilometres. Most of the energy used in flight goes into keeping the insect in the air, while only a small proportion is used to propel the insect forward. In both butterflies and moths, the fore- and hindwings work together (in different ways) to operate as a single pair of flexible wings. Dainty Swallowtails (*Papilio anactus*) use both pairs of wings when actively flying but use mainly the hindwings when hovering over flowers.

The veins of butterfly and moth wings reinforce the whole structure. The membranes in between, only a thousandth of a millimetre thick, allow bending and flattening at different parts of the wing stroke. Many butterflies are remarkable in that their wings meet at the top and bottom of the wing stroke (called a "clap and peel" motion), which accelerates wing wear and causes loss of scales over time.

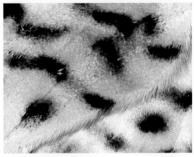

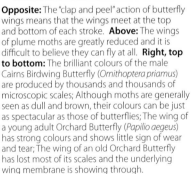

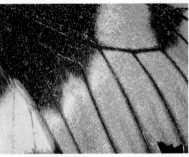

**Opposite:** The "clap and peel" action of butterfly wings means that the wings meet at the top and bottom of each stroke. **Above:** The wings of plume moths are greatly reduced and it is difficult to believe they can fly at all. **Right, top to bottom:** The brilliant colours of the male Cairns Birdwing Butterfly (*Ornithoptera priamus*) are produced by thousands and thousands of microscopic scales; Although moths are generally seen as dull and brown, their colours can be just as spectacular as those of butterflies; The wing of a young adult Orchard Butterfly (*Papilio aegeus*) has strong colours and shows little sign of wear and tear; The wing of an old Orchard Butterfly has lost most of its scales and the underlying wing membrane is showing through.

# Finding Food

Caterpillars feed on leaves and other parts of the plant, such as fruits and flowers. They have chewing mouthparts and most species spend almost their entire time as caterpillars doing nothing but feeding. In some cases, every leaf on a plant will be stripped. In 1957 the Gum Leaf Skeletoniser (*Uraba lugens*) exfoliated gum trees over 40,000 hectares in Victoria. The presence of insects may have a detrimental effect on plants. The dung dropped by insects feeding on gum trees has chemicals in it that suppress germination and growth of the seedlings below.

All of the nutrients required for building and sustaining an adult butterfly or moth are gathered by the caterpillar. As the eggs are usually laid on the leaves of the food plant, caterpillars do not need strategies to actively find food.

## FIGHTING BACK

In response to this onslaught, plants defend themselves in a number of ways. Mechanical means include tough leaves, which wear down the caterpillars' mouthparts. Some plants are able to starve insects of essential nutrients such as nitrogen. The majority of plants, often in conjunction with mechanical defences, protect themselves using chemicals. These chemicals are a complex and varied group of compounds, which serve to deter, repel, sterilise or kill the caterpillars, or (more subtly) to slow down their growth.

Some caterpillars can neutralise toxic compounds by turning them into a harmless chemical or by breaking them down. Insects such as the toxic Wanderer Butterfly (*Danaus plexippus*) absorb the plant's defences and use them as their own.

## LIKE A BUTTERFLY TO NECTAR

A remarkable number of moth species have no mouthparts and cannot feed. Butterflies, however, feed on flower nectar, which is basically liquid sugar. Having consumed all the necessary proteins and other nutrients as caterpillars, the adults require only energy from sugar to continue flying.

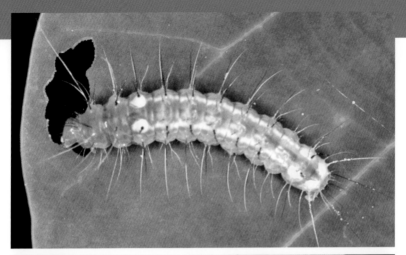

**Opposite, top to bottom:** This female Cairns Birdwing Butterfly is covered with orange pollen picked up feeding at flowers; Moths and butterflies tend to feed only from flowers with a particular structure that suits their long proboscises. **Above, top to bottom:** Each type of caterpillar feeds in a particular way. Some only scrape off the leaf surface, others chew the entire leaf; Many butterflies will feed on bird droppings, particularly those of fruit-eating birds.

# Natural Enemies

Butterflies and moths are attacked by a wide range of natural enemies, but by far the biggest threat is parasitic attack against the caterpillars. Other enemies include vertebrates, such as birds, and invertebrates, such as spiders, as well as fungi and diseases.

## THE EARLY BIRD

Most vertebrates include insects in at least some part of their diet. Even nectar-feeding birds require the protein that insects provide. Birds scour entire plants for the few caterpillars they may find there and entire families of birds are adept at capturing butterflies on the wing. Moths make up a large part of the diet of bats, which use echolocation (using echoes to "see" their surroundings) to detect them in the dark.

## VEGETABLE CATERPILLARS

There are also a number of types of fungi, particularly *Cordyceps* species, that attack and kill caterpillars living underground. The fungus replaces all of the host insect's tissues with its own, resulting in a caterpillar-shaped fungus (called a vegetable caterpillar) that sends out fruiting bodies, which release spores that go on to infect other hosts. Some caterpillars are able to fight back against fungal attacks by isolating the spores within the body and eliminating them.

## THE CATERPILLAR FLU

Like humans and other animals, butterflies and moths suffer from bacteria, viruses and other disease-causing agents, particularly in the caterpillar stage. Most of these are specific to particular species and cannot infect other organisms such as humans. Many species are attacked by a virus called a Nuclear Polyhedral Virus, which turns its host into a bag of virus-filled fluid and may survive more than ten years outside the host, ready to infect a new host caterpillar as soon as the virus is consumed.

## THE ENEMY WITHIN

Most caterpillars are attacked by at least one species of parasitic fly or wasp. These parasites are tiny, often too small to see, and lay their eggs within the bodies of their hosts. The parasitic larva feeds on the caterpillar's internal tissues, avoiding the vital organs so that the host can continue living and feeding. When fully fed, the parasitic larva pupates and eventually emerges as an adult, leaving behind a dead caterpillar and flying off to find new hosts.

**Opposite:** Spiders and birds are the main predators of butterflies. Despite the protective covering of scales, many butterflies become trapped in spider webs. **Above, clockwise from top left:** A Ulysses Butterfly caterpillar subspecies (*Papilio ulysses joesea*) killed by a virus. The caterpillar's body is now a bag of virus-filled fluid; An Orchard Butterfly caterpillar (*Papilio aegeus*) killed by a Nuclear Polyhedral Virus, showing the characteristic limp body still attached to the leaf; The small, white eggs of a parasitic fly can be seen just behind the head of this cup moth caterpillar; This Cabbage White Butterfly caterpillar (*Pieris rapae*) is now an empty shell, completely filled with cocoons of the parasitic wasps that consumed it; This moth caterpillar has been eaten by wasp parasites, which have left their victim and spun white cocoons on the outside.

# Defensive Strategies

Under the onslaught of their natural enemies, butterflies and moths employ a range of defensive strategies. The most common method is to rapidly leave the scene — caterpillars do so by dropping off the leaf; butterflies do so with fast and erratic flight; many moths fall to the ground and feign death. Many caterpillars sport spines, stinging hairs or bristles, which release chemicals on contact, others regurgitate a sticky fluid or thrash around wildly to scare off predators. A number of moth caterpillars, such as the Hercules Moth (*Coscinocera hercules*), cover themselves with wax to clog up predators' mouthparts.

### HIDING IN THE OPEN

Some species have modified their shape, pattern and colour scheme to make themselves disappear altogether — this is called camouflage. Camouflage involves the use of colour, body shape and behaviour to resemble leaves, flowers, bark or stones. The caterpillars of snout moths have brown, mottled markings and lines of hairs on the sides of the body, which blend the outline into a branch, removing any potential shadows. Adult looper moths are renowned for their broad flattened wings, which perfectly blur the outline between the wings and the background.

### LIVING BIRD POO

Another strategy employed by caterpillars is to pretend to be something else — this is called mimicry. In its early stages, the Orchard Butterfly caterpillar (*Papilio aegeus*) is marked with brown and white, closely resembling a fresh bird dropping. Once they become too large to continue with this strategy, the caterpillars become green and are beautifully camouflaged amid the green foliage.

### BUILDING PROTECTION

To protect themselves from predators, parasites and bad weather, many caterpillars build shelters from materials in their environment. The Saunders' Case Moth caterpillar (*Oiketicus elongatus*) weaves a silken bag that is covered in sticks to camouflage and protect itself. Although extremely tough, the bag can be torn open by persistent shrike-tits (*Falcunculus* spp.) and the caterpillars are regularly attacked by parasitic wasps. Other caterpillars weave silken shelters by sewing together leaves or constructing retreats made from silk interwoven with their own frass (droppings).

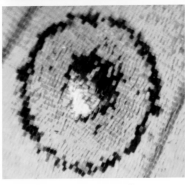

**Opposite:** Hercules Moth caterpillars are not only covered with spines, but possess a thick layer of wax when young. **Top:** Swallowtail caterpillars have a smelly, fleshy organ behind the head, which appears when the caterpillar is disturbed. **Above, left to right:** Many species of butterflies and moths bear "eyespots" on the wings to frighten off predators; Behind the head, Ulysses Butterfly caterpillars (*Papilio ulysses joesea*) have a blue eyespot that is concealed until the caterpillar is disturbed.

# Conservation

The most serious threat to butterflies and moths in Australia is loss of habitat. Most species rely on native plants for their survival, both as food for the caterpillars and food for the adults. If plants are cleared from an area, the butterflies and moths must disappear as well. In many parts of New South Wales, Victoria, Queensland, South Australia and Western Australia, native habitats have been cleared to make way for pasture and other forms of farming. Only very small pockets of native vegetation survive, host to tiny remnant populations of butterflies and moths. The most seriously threatened species are those that rely on native grasslands.

Other threats to butterfly and moth populations include pesticides, pollution, weeds and introduced animals. Butterfly collectors sometimes capture large numbers of butterflies, but this does not appear to have a severe impact on the overall population. Butterfly and moth populations play an essential role in the ecology of all terrestrial environments and are important components of most food chains.

## FIGHTING BACK

Insect conservation has been an accepted issue in Europe and North America for many years, but only really "grew wings" in Australia in the late 1980s, when the campaign began to save the Eltham Copper Butterfly (*Paralucia pyrodiscus*) from habitat loss caused by a housing development near Melbourne. Recovery plans have also been implemented for the Altona Skipper (*Hesperilla flavescens*) in Melbourne and the Bathurst Copper (*Paralucia spinifera*) in New South Wales. In South-East Queensland, an awareness campaign about the plight of the Richmond Birdwing (*Ornithoptera richmondia*) has resulted in local schools, community groups and government authorities becoming involved in its conservation and recovery.

Moths attract less interest than butterflies, but the threatened status of the Golden Sun Moth (*Synemon plana*) has received considerable attention since the 1990s. This species lives in native grasslands, which have been reduced to a very small percentage of their original distribution due to habitat clearing and introduced pasture. It is now protected over parts of its range and attempts are underway to reintroduce it to areas where it no longer exists.

**Left:** Suitable host plants have been planted in areas where Ulysses Swallowtails were once rare, drawing these butterflies back to their former habitats.

**Above, clockwise from top:** The Cairns
Birdwing Butterfly (*Ornithoptera euphorion*) is
totally dependent on the *Aristolochia* vine for its
continued survival; An Eltham Copper Butterfly
caterpillar feeding at night with its attendant
ants; The natural range of Golden Sun Moths
has become greatly diminished as native host
grasses have disappeared; Many species of
native butterflies are now living in suburban
areas as gardeners plant suitable host plants.

# Butterflies

Butterflies are probably the best known and most loved group of insects in the world. Whereas many insect groups are described only to the genus level, butterflies are often known by their subspecies, seasonal forms and individual populations. Despite being the most researched insects in Australia, there are undoubtedly a number of species yet to be discovered. However, the known number of species, at 416, is tiny in comparison to the number of moths known to science.

All butterflies possess two pairs of wings and, unlike moths, there are no wingless species. For feeding, under the head they also possess a coiled proboscis, which is absent in many moth species. Butterflies are often considered to be day-flying moths, as they are a small, colourful sub-branch of the moth tree of life. Like moths, they are essential components of natural systems and are important pollinators. Nearly half the butterfly species in Australia are found in rainforests and many species are undoubtedly involved in pollinating a number of rainforest plants.

**Top:** All butterflies drink through a proboscis, which is rolled up under the head when not in use. **Above, left to right:** The wings of some butterflies are covered with scales, the colour of which changes depending on the angle of the light; A Brown Soldier (*Junonia hedonia*) emerging from its pupa. The crumpled wings will take several hours to dry before the butterfly can fly off. **Opposite:** Although they have rather large eyes, most caterpillars have poor eyesight.

# Skippers

**Family: Hesperiidae**

Skippers are a family of small to medium-sized butterflies, characterised by stout bodies and short wings. Wingspan varies between 18–58 mm. Most species have yellow-brown patterns on the wings, sometimes with dark brown or black markings. Very few species are brilliantly coloured. Skippers occupy a diverse range of habitats, from forests to swamplands.

Adult skippers fly rapidly and often erratically, usually close to the ground. They prefer to fly in bright sunshine and stop regularly to feed at flowers. Many species are territorial, with the males patrolling precisely determined areas in search of females. A male will have a particular perch, such as a prominent twig, to which he always returns after patrolling. If the male disappears, another male may take over his territory and will usually sit on the same twig. Adults mate end to end, facing opposite directions while resting on the plant. The eggs are relatively large and are laid singly on the leaves of food plants.

The caterpillars have a prominent head and a body that tapers at each end. They generally feed at night on a wide range of food plants, including sedges and reeds. During the day they construct shelters by sewing together two or more leaves of the food plant with silk, or hide in leaf litter at the base of the plant.

There are 124 species of skipper in Australia and more than 3500 species worldwide. Of these, 77 species are found only in Australia.

**Top:** Skippers are found all over the world, except New Zealand. Australia has a particularly rich butterfly fauna. **Right:** Although most skippers are brown or yellow, a range of other colour variations can be found.

# Symmomus Skipper *Trapezites symmomus*

*Males of this species occupy territories around food plants. During the morning they patrol along the ground, searching for females. In the afternoon, males establish territories in nearby trees, which they defend vigorously.*

DESCRIPTION: Like most skipper species, Symmomus Skippers are brown with yellow and orange markings. Males and females are very difficult to distinguish but females have more rounded wings than males.

LIFE HISTORY: The female lays creamy white eggs with reddish-brown patches singly on or near the base of food plants, which consist of five species of mat rush. Young caterpillars make a shelter by joining two leaves together with silk; older caterpillars make a silk-lined tubular shelter by rolling up a living or dead leaf. The caterpillar grows up to 40 mm long and is pinkish-brown with a dark line down the back and a reddish-brown head. The fully fed caterpillar pupates within the shelter or at the base of the food plant and is up to 30 mm long and pale brown with dark spots. In most of the range there is only one generation per year, but there may be two in South-East Queensland and New South Wales.

BEHAVIOUR: Like other skippers, this species prefers to fly in bright sunshine in the mornings, particularly around flowers. The flying period ranges from August–April in Queensland to January–March in Victoria.

HABITAT: Found in dry forest, woodlands, heathlands, swamplands and rainforest edges.

DISTRIBUTION: Coastal Qld, NSW, eastern Victoria.

SIZE: Male wingspan is 42 mm; female wingspan is 46 mm.

*This species, although small, is well travelled. It is found in wet rainforests in north Queensland and the Torres Strait islands, as well as mainland New Guinea and associated islands.*

**DESCRIPTION:** Banded Demons can be distinguished by a large white band on the forewing. The spots near the tip of the forewing are larger in the female than the male. The male usually has three spots and the female five spots, but both are variable.

**LIFE HISTORY:** The eggs have not been recorded but are probably large and smooth, in the shape of a semi-circle. The caterpillars are pale green with a dark brown head and feed on Native Ginger. They feed at night and rest during the day in a cylindrical shelter lined with silk, formed by the caterpillar cutting and rolling a leaf of the food plant. When it has finished feeding, it constructs another shelter in a rolled leaf near the base of the plant and pupates suspended within.

**BEHAVIOUR:** Adults fly throughout the year and are often seen feeding from flowers, moving between them with a short, swift flight. When resting, they hold their wings above them but may open them when feeding or basking in the sun.

**HABITAT:** They are found in rainforest and drier monsoon forest where their food plants occur. They are common within their habitat but rare in other parts of their range.

**DISTRIBUTION:** Coastal north Qld, from Paluma northwards.

**SIZE:** Male wingspan is 35 mm; female wingspan is 38 mm.

# Swallowtails
## Family: Papilionidae

The name "swallowtail" is derived from members of this family, particularly in Europe, that have "tails" arising from the hindwings. Few Australian species have such tails. Most swallowtails are large and boldly patterned. The world's largest butterflies belong to this group, including the Cairns Birdwing Butterfly (*Ornithoptera priamus*), which is the largest butterfly in Australia. Swallowtails' wingspans vary between 48–150 mm. They are found in a range of habitats across Australia, but mostly within 200 km of the coast. This family is most abundant in tropical areas.

Adults fly strongly and some species undertake migrations. They feed frequently at flowers, often with the wings held up behind the body and vibrating slightly. Males in particular may congregate in puddles or at stream edges to drink water. They also fly around the tops of hills, patrolling for females (called hilltopping). Mating may take several hours and the female often flies around with the male hanging below. The eggs are round and usually attached singly to the leaves of the food plants.

The caterpillars are generally spiky when young but may become smooth-bodied later on. Behind the head is a brightly-coloured, fleshy organ (called the osmeterium), which may produce a strong smell and is used for defence. The caterpillars are often well camouflaged and feed openly during the day on the leaves of food plants that include members of the citrus, carrot and laurel families.

There are eighteen swallowtail species in Australia and more than 560 species worldwide.

**Top:** The Ambrax Butterfly (*Papilio ambrax*) is one of seventeen species of swallowtail found in the Australian region. **Left:** Swallowtail caterpillars tend to be large, colourful and fleshy, often with soft spines along the body.

*The female Cairns Birdwing Butterfly is the largest butterfly in Australia and one of the largest in the world. Most birdwing species live in New Guinea, where the world's largest butterfly, the Queen Alexandra Birdwing, also lives.*

**DESCRIPTION:** The female (below) is brown-black with creamy-white markings. Males (above) have extensive green-blue and yellow markings. There is great variation in the wing pattern of this species. Males may occasionally be blue instead of green, although this is rare, and females are occasionally more creamy white than black.

**LIFE HISTORY:** The round, yellow eggs are laid singly by the female on the undersides of the leaves of food plants, which include nine species of *Aristolochia*. The caterpillars vary from black-brown to brown-grey with rows of long spines. They grow to 64 mm long and feed alone on the food plant. Fully fed caterpillars will often ringbark the plant before pupating, which causes the remaining leaves to die and enhances the pupa's camouflage. The pupa is 50 mm long, golden-brown with yellow markings and attached to the plant by a silken girdle. The life cycle takes 2–3 months.

**BEHAVIOUR:** Adults fly throughout the year with a gliding flight, often at the tops of trees. Courtship lasts up to fifteen minutes with the male hovering just below and behind the female. Mating may last several hours.

**HABITAT:** Found in rainforest, sometimes dry forest and suburban areas where the food plant is present.

**DISTRIBUTION:** Coastal north Qld.

**SIZE:** Male wingspan is 125 mm; female wingspan is 150 mm.

# Orchard Butterfly *Papilio aegeus*

*There are three forms of the female Orchard Butterfly in Australia, including a very pale form found only in north Queensland. This form, called the Iron Range Orchard, has forewings that are almost completely white.*

**DESCRIPTION:** Males and females have similar colours but males have much more black on the wings than females. Both sexes have small patches of red around the edges of the hindwings.

**LIFE HISTORY:** The female lays pale yellow eggs singly on the leaves and shoots of food plants, which include 40 species in the citrus family, most notably Citruswood and Leopardwood. Young caterpillars are brown and white with a remarkable resemblance to fresh bird droppings. Caterpillars feed singly during the day and rest at night. Older caterpillars grow to 62 mm and are green with irregular yellowish-white markings edged with brown. The pupa is up to 40 mm long and varies from bluish-green to grey with brown markings, depending in part on the location of the plant.

**BEHAVIOUR:** Adults fly throughout the year in Queensland but only from October–May in New South Wales. Their flight is slow and erratic, with the butterflies stopping frequently to feed at flowers. The male hovers above the female during courtship and mating may take several hours.

**HABITAT:** They occur across many habitats, from moist lowland rainforest to dry woodlands and suburban areas.

**DISTRIBUTION:** Coastal Qld, NSW, parts of Vic, SA and NT.

**SIZE:** Male wingspan is 102 mm; female wingspan is 108 mm.

**Top:** Orchard Butterfly caterpillars change colour as they grow. The older stages are mostly green and are well camouflaged among leaves of the food plant. **Below, left to right:** Unlike females, male Orchard Butterflies are mostly black with only small areas of white; Female Orchard Butterflies are most commonly seen at citrus trees, hovering around the flowers or laying eggs.

*Chequered Swallowtails migrate over various regions of Australia, depending on local conditions. Large numbers of butterflies are sometimes involved, flying rapidly up to seven metres per second. They are also found from Iran through India to Malaysia and New Guinea.*

**DESCRIPTION:** Adults are black with pale yellow spots and larger pale areas near the base of the wings. There is also a blue spot and orange-brown spot on opposite sides of the hindwings. The underside is similar but with large areas of pale yellow and more extensive orange-brown markings. Young caterpillars are mostly black with green markings, becoming paler green with age.

**LIFE HISTORY:** The eggs are laid singly on the leaves of food plants. Caterpillars feed on a range of *Cullen* and *Psoralea* species as well as on citrus plants. They feed exposed during the day and rest frequently on the stems. When finished feeding, they pupate attached to a stem or at the base of the plant.

Development takes three to six weeks and the pupal stage varies from sixteen days to ten months.

**BEHAVIOUR:** Adults fly very rapidly during the day, usually only a couple of metres from the ground. They are often seen feeding at flowers or puddles.

**HABITAT:** They are found in a range of habitats where the food plants grow, from moist gullies to semi-arid areas.

**DISTRIBUTION:** All States and Territories except Tasmania.

**SIZE:** Male wingspan is 72 mm; female wingspan is 75 mm.

**Below:** When feeding or resting, an adult Chequered Swallowtail holds its wings high up behind its body. **Bottom:** The contrasting colours of the adults make this one of the most attractive butterfly species in Australia.

# Ulysses Swallowtail   *Papilio ulysses*

*The Ulysses Swallowtail is one of the most brightly coloured butterflies in Australia. The blue is impossible to represent in photographs or drawings, as it is generated in a different way to most other colours in the world.*

**DESCRIPTION:** The male has six patches of dull-grey scales among the black on the outer edges of the forewings. The female has a series of small blue patches among the black on the bottom edges of the hindwings.

**LIFE HISTORY:** The female lays yellow-green eggs singly on young leaves of food plants, which include Pink Euodia and related species, such as Leopardwood. The caterpillar feeds on young foliage of smaller trees. Young caterpillars are yellow with blue-black markings, while older caterpillars are dark green with thick white bands and spots. The pupa is 38 mm long, varying in colour from pale green to pinkish-brown. It hangs by a girdle underneath a leaf or branch of the food plant. Adults fly throughout the year but are most common during the wet season.

**BEHAVIOUR:** Adults fly in an erratic zig-zag fashion through the rainforest canopy, feeding at flowers such as Lantana. Males are attracted, sometimes over long distances, by bright blue colours. They close the wings at rest and are very difficult to see.

**HABITAT:** They live in rainforest and suburban areas, particularly wet upland areas, and may be especially common in areas of rainforest regrowth.

**DISTRIBUTION:** Found throughout north Queensland, in patches from Sarina northwards.

**SIZE:** Male wingspan is 106 mm; female wingspan is 108 mm.

**Below and right:** In contrast to the upper surface of the wings, the lower surface is dull brown.

# Whites & Yellows
## Family: Pieridae

Members of this family, also known as pierids, are small to medium-sized butterflies that are mostly white and yellow but may also be red, black and orange. Most members of the family have special pigments called pterines that produce the characteristic yellows and whites. Wingspan varies between 29–72 mm.

They are generally found in the tropics, particularly within rainforests. Few species occur in southern Australia and none in Tasmania other than the introduced Cabbage White Butterfly (*Pieris rapae*). Adults feed on nectar from a range of flowers.

Larger species may be strong fliers but the smaller yellows fly erratically close to the ground. Flight is strongly stimulated by sunlight and many species quickly settle when it becomes cloudy. More than half the Australian species demonstrate migratory habits, particularly in eastern Australia. Thousands of butterflies may travel together for days on end, but the purpose of most migrations is unknown.

Adults mate end to end, with wings overlapping, while standing on a branch or leaf. The eggs are narrow, tall and ribbed, either white or yellow. They are laid singly or in batches of up to 50. Caterpillars are generally green to reddish-brown, with slender bodies that do not have spines. They feed on a vast range of food plants from many different plant families. Most species feed singly but some feed in groups.

Australia has 35 species that belong to the Pieridae family, but there are more than 1000 species worldwide.

**Top:** The Caper White Butterfly undergoes massive migrations in most years.

*Vast numbers of Caper White adults may migrate southwards in spring over large areas, sometimes reaching southern Tasmania and remaining for several weeks. At night they rest in groups on bushes. The adults feed on flowers along the way, but do not breed down south as there are no suitable host plants.*

**DESCRIPTION:** Males and females are very similar but the females have more black on the wings than the males. Females are highly variable, from very pale forms to very dark ones. In the dark form, the yellow areas are also larger and brighter.

**LIFE HISTORY:** The female lays clusters of yellow-orange eggs (in groups of up to 100) on the leaves and stems of food plants, which are mainly caper species. Young caterpillars eat large quantities of leaf, leaving only the midvein. Older caterpillars consume the whole leaf and may defoliate entire plants. They grow to 32 mm long and vary from olive-green to brown, with raised yellow spots supporting numerous white hairs. The pupa, which may be 25 mm long, hangs underneath a leaf or stem and is mottled white with patches of black.

**BEHAVIOUR:** Males patrol continuously around food plants or clusters of pupae and will mate with females soon after they emerge.

**HABITAT:** They live in a number of habitats, but prefer inland areas west of the Great Dividing Range, where their food plants are present.

**DISTRIBUTION:** Found in all States and Territories. This species is migratory and its presence in southern NSW, Vic, ACT, Tas and SA is generally only temporary.

**SIZE:** Both the male and female wingspan is 55 mm.

*Although these are small butterflies and apparently weak fliers, adults are occasionally found on offshore islands, having flown up to 60 km across the tops of the waves.*

**DESCRIPTION:** The upperside of the female's wings is sprinkled with black scales, which may be absent in the male. Otherwise they are very difficult to tell apart. There are also a few other species that look very similar.

**LIFE HISTORY:** The female lays tiny white eggs singly on leaves of the food plants, which include twenty species of snow bush, senna and wattles. The caterpillar is dull green with a fine white line down each side, and grows up to 30 mm long. Fully fed caterpillars pupate under a branch of the food plant, held on by a silken girdle. The pupa is 20 mm long and bright green.

Adults fly throughout the year and there are several generations per year, taking as little as three weeks from egg to adult, depending on temperature. In Sydney, the life cycle takes significantly longer than further north. They are most common during autumn and winter in the tropics.

**BEHAVIOUR:** Adults fly close to the ground with a slow, erratic flight, stopping occasionally to feed at flowers. Adults may migrate some distance when food plants become scarce.

**HABITAT:** Found in dry forests and savanna woodlands, usually wherever the food plants are found.

**DISTRIBUTION:** Qld, NSW, north-west WA, northern NT.

**SIZE:** Male wingspan is 37 mm; female wingspan is 40 mm.

*This species was introduced in 1929 and is the only serious butterfly pest in Australia. Its caterpillars feed on more than 150 species of plants. A number of parasitic wasps have been introduced in attempts to control it.*

**DESCRIPTION:** Adults vary in colour from pure white to a pale creamy yellow. The female has two black spots on the forewings but the male has only one spot.

**LIFE HISTORY:** The female produces large numbers of pale yellow eggs on the undersides of the leaves of the food plant. The caterpillar grows to 20 mm long and is green with a faint yellow line down the back. Older caterpillars are voracious feeders and can defoliate entire plants, causing problems for commercial growers. Food plants include cabbages, cauliflowers, broccoli and turnips, as well as Tick Weeds, woad species and Canary Creeper. The pupa is 18 mm long, green or grey-brown and usually located away from the food plant. Adults fly throughout the year and are often the only butterfly seen during winter in southern Australia, where there may be up to five generations per year.

**BEHAVIOUR:** Adults fly erratically and stop frequently to feed at flowers. The male flies just below and behind the female during courtship. They mate side by side.

**HABITAT:** Found in suburban areas and farmland as well as natural bushland.

**DISTRIBUTION:** South-East Qld, NSW, Vic, Tas, south-eastern SA, plus scattered occurrences in north Qld, NT and WA.

**SIZE:** Both the male and female wingspan is 44 mm.

*Male Imperial White Butterflies often fly around hilltops (behaviour common to many butterfly species), setting up territories and patrolling for passing females. Females visit the hilltops to select the most suitable male to mate with.*

**DESCRIPTION:** The upperside of the wings is dull white bordered with black and with white spots near the tips. The undersides of the wings are largely black with red and yellow spots. There are two forms, which appear in summer–autumn and winter–spring, with the spring form more grey than white.

**LIFE HISTORY:** The eggs are laid in clusters of up to 100 on the leaves of the food plants. The caterpillars feed in groups on a range of mistletoe species, spreading sheets of silk over the leaves as they feed. Up to 70 caterpillars may be found on a single mistletoe. When they have finished feeding, the caterpillars spin further sheets of silk over the trunk or a branch and pupate in a group. Caterpillars that pupate in summer are usually orange and those that pupate in winter are black.

**BEHAVIOUR:** Adults are not commonly seen as they fly around the tree tops where the mistletoes grow. On very hot days they cease flying and gather together in cool gullies. Adults fly throughout the year but are less common in winter.

**HABITAT:** These butterflies live mostly in eucalypt forests, where their food plants are common.

**DISTRIBUTION:** Along the Great Dividing Range and coastal areas of NSW and Vic.

**SIZE:** Male wingspan is 67 mm; female wingspan is 72 mm.

# Nymphs
## Family: Nymphalidae

Nymphs are a family of basically brown butterflies ranging in size from small to large. The family is also given the common name of "browns", although there are some particularly colourful species. Wingspan varies between 28–95 mm. The forelegs are small in all species and are never used for walking, being held up against the thorax.

Nymphs are found in most terrestrial habitats in Australia. Unlike other butterfly families, this one is more diverse in species in southern Australia than in the tropics.

Some species favour flying in bright sunshine or bask in the sun with their wings outstretched, while others stay in the shade. Some species are weak fliers and spend most of their time roosting; others are very strong fliers and migrate across oceans. Adults feed actively at the flowers of numerous plant species and some may be important pollinators.

Mating takes place end to end. The egg is variable in shape and colour but is most commonly round. The caterpillars are very diverse in shape and size and the pupae always hang downwards, usually from a leaf or branch of the host plant. Most caterpillars of this family feed at night and conceal themselves during the day, but some species feed openly on plants in the daytime. The caterpillars eat a variety of host plants, particularly small annual species and grasses.

There are 81 nymph species in Australia, with more than 6000 species worldwide.

**Top:** Like many nymph butterflies, the Bordered Rustic (*Cupha prosope*) has a background colour of yellow and brown.  **Right:** The Cape York Hamadryad (*Tellervo zoilus*) is a small but very attractive butterfly found in rainforests.

The Swamp Tiger has possibly more than 30 subspecies spread throughout Thailand, the Philippines and Indonesia. Two of these occur in Australia, but only one in the Torres Strait islands. A subspecies (D. a. affinis) is also known as the Marsh Tiger or Black and White Tiger.

**DESCRIPTION:** The upperside of the wings is mostly brown-black with areas of white in the centre of the wings and white spots around the edges. The sexes are very similar to each other. The caterpillar is dark blue with three white spots across the body at each segment. Pairs of black fleshy filaments arise from the front and back end of the body.

**LIFE HISTORY:** The cream coloured eggs are laid singly on leaves of the food plant, which is a climbing vine called Mangrove Milkweed. Caterpillars will strip all of the leaves before pupating head downwards on nearby reeds. The pupa is smooth and pale green to pink, with four golden spots near the base. Adults are on the wing throughout the year and appear to breed continuously.

**BEHAVIOUR:** Adults fly slowly within a few metres of the ground, stopping regularly to feed at flowers. They settle frequently on low branches but roost higher up in the trees at night.

**HABITAT:** They prefer wet habitats, such as brackish creeks and mangrove swamps, where their food plants are found.

**DISTRIBUTION:** Coastal Qld and the northern half of NSW, as well as the Top End of NT.

**SIZE:** Male wingspan is 65 mm; female wingspan is 62 mm.

# Wanderer Butterfly   *Danaus plexippus*

*This species was originally found only in North and South America, where it is known as the Monarch. In the 1800s, however, it spread across the Pacific to Hawaii and eventually to Australia, assisted by the prevailing winds.*

**DESCRIPTION:** Adults are orange-brown on both the upper and lower surfaces of the wings, with thick black veins. The body and edges of the wings are black, speckled with white dots. Near the centre of the hindwing, the males have a black patch of sex-scales, which are absent in the females. The caterpillars are striped yellow, white and black across the body.

**LIFE HISTORY:** The long white eggs are laid singly on leaves of food plants, which comprise introduced swan plants or milkweeds. The caterpillars are voracious feeders and may strip entire plants of leaves. In some areas they are heavily parasitised by Tachinid flies.

They usually leave the food plant to pupate. The pupa is smooth and pale green, with a series of gold dots near the top. It becomes transparent just before the adult emerges. Where permanent populations exist, adults are on the wing throughout the year.

**BEHAVIOUR:** Adults have a graceful, gliding flight. Males patrol around patches of the food plants, awaiting the females, which tend to visit briefly to mate and lay eggs.

**HABITAT:** Suburban gardens and grasslands suit this species, which lives wherever food plants are found.

**DISTRIBUTION:** Permanent populations occur on the Qld coast and isolated areas around Sydney, Adelaide and Perth. Temporary populations may arise across south-east Australia and Tasmania.

**SIZE:** Male wingspan is 93 mm; female wingspan is 92 mm.

**Below:** The Wanderer pupa (right) is bright green with gold spots when new, but the adult's wings (below) begin to show through just before emergence.

*This is a common and widespread species that is most abundant after the end of the wet season. It is also called the Oleander Butterfly, as its caterpillars feed on the introduced Oleander, particularly when grown as street trees.*

DESCRIPTION: The sexes are very similar, but males have a thin horizontal patch of silky scales in the middle of the forewing.

LIFE HISTORY: The pale yellow eggs are laid singly on the underside of the leaves and flowers of food plants. The caterpillars feed on more than 50 species of food plants, most notably figs and the introduced Oleander. Fully grown caterpillars are 57 mm long, orange-brown with black bands across the body and four pairs of long, black, fleshy filaments. The pupa is 18 mm long and very variable in colour, from silver to brown and gold, sometimes with darker markings. The time from egg to adult is about one month. Adults feed on a wide range of flowers. They fly throughout the year but spend the dry season in very large aggregations in shaded gullies, overhanging rocks, cave entrances and offshore islands.

BEHAVIOUR: The adults have a slow, sailing flight a few metres off the ground and stop regularly to feed at flowers.

HABITAT: Found in open forests, woodlands, monsoon forests, rainforest edges and suburban areas, particularly where Oleanders have been planted in gardens and on nature strips.

DISTRIBUTION: Qld, northern WA, northern NT. Occurs across the top of Australia but is occasionally found in NSW and even Vic.

SIZE: Male wingspan is 69 mm; female wingspan is 72 mm.

*The pupa of this species has three brilliant gold spots on its back — these may be to break up the outline of the pupa and help it avoid detection from predators by making it resemble dappled sunlight filtering through the foliage.*

**DESCRIPTION:** The female is very similar to the male but the orange on the upperside of her wing is more orange-brown and her abdomen is more brown than orange.

**LIFE HISTORY:** The yellow eggs are laid in clusters of up to 40 on the leaves of the food plant, which is the tropical Lacewing Vine (*Adenia heterophylla*). The vine grows in monsoon forest, often reaching high into the canopy. Caterpillars grow up to 32 mm and are striped white, orange and black, with numerous soft, black spines. They feed together in groups when young and later cluster together along the stems of the food plant. They can consume vast quantities of leaves and stems before pupating together, hanging head downwards from stems. The pupa is bluish-black with white mottling and gold spots. The adults fly throughout the year but are most abundant from April to July.

**BEHAVIOUR:** Adults fly in sunlit patches of rainforest and frequently settle on the ground, where courtship and mating takes place. They also spend time basking in the sun on leaves where possible.

**HABITAT:** Patches of monsoon forest, particularly along streams, where their food plants are common.

**DISTRIBUTION:** North coastal NT.

**SIZE:** Male wingspan is 65 mm; female wingspan is 67 mm.

**Above and right:**
Common Browns often
rest on the ground where
they are very difficult to see.

*This species is very common and widespread in south-eastern Australia, where it is perhaps the most abundant butterfly in the region. At certain times of year, clouds of butterflies inhabit vast areas of grassy woodlands.*

**DESCRIPTION:** Both sexes are brownish-orange with black markings, but the female has much more black on the forewing than the male.

**LIFE HISTORY:** The cream-coloured eggs are laid singly on leaves of the food plant, which includes eight species of grasses such as Kangaroo Grass. Fully grown caterpillars are 36 mm long, varying in colour from green to pinkish-brown, mottled with darker brown, depending in part on the condition of the food plant. The pupa is 18 mm long, brown and mottled with darker spots and is placed among leaf litter in a shallow cavity lined with silk. There is one generation per year but the flying period may cover eight months, from September to May, in some areas.

**BEHAVIOUR:** Adults fly slowly, stopping to feed on a range of flowers and occasionally settling on the ground where they are very difficult to see. Males fly close to the ground over grasses early in the season, but later fly higher in the canopy and are common on the tops of hills, where they court passing females.

**HABITAT:** They occupy diverse habitats in both coastal and mountainous areas. They are most common in grassy woodland and open eucalypt forest.

**DISTRIBUTION:** South-East Qld, NSW, Vic, Tas, south-east SA, south-west WA.

**SIZE:** Male wingspan is 56 mm; female wingspan is 64 mm.

# Blue-banded Eggfly *Hypolimnas alimena*

*There is some evidence that this species can hybridise with the Common Eggfly, as their ranges are almost identical. The resulting adult females look like Common Eggflies but have much more blue on the wings than orange.*

**DESCRIPTION:** The sexes are similar, however, near the tip of the forewing, the female has a broken band of four white spots, which are absent in the male.

**LIFE HISTORY:** The female lays pale blue-green eggs singly on leaves of the food plant, mainly the native *Pseuderanthemum* and the introduced *Asystasia* species. The eggs hatch in a few days. The caterpillar is black with many branched spines and a dark brown head. They feed at night and sometimes during the day and may shelter among debris near the food plant. The pupa is brown-black, mottled with grey, and hangs head downwards in a sheltered spot near the food plant. Adults fly throughout the year in north Queensland but are most common during and shortly after the wet season. There are several generations per year in the north.

**BEHAVIOUR:** Males (below) are territorial and will perch on foliage in sunlight or on an open patch of ground to await passing females. Females tend to fly close to the ground in search of plants on which to lay eggs.

**HABITAT:** Prefers rainforest, particularly lowland rainforest edges, where their food plant grows along the ground.

**DISTRIBUTION:** Qld, NSW, NT. There are two subspecies — one found around the Darwin area and the other along the Qld coast from the tip of Cape York to northern NSW.

**SIZE:** Male wingspan is 69 mm; female wingspan is 67 mm.

# Common Eggfly  *Hypolimnas bolina*

*This species sometimes flies all the way from Australia to New Zealand, where it is known locally as the Blue Moon. The right food plants are not present there, however, so Common Eggflies do not breed there.*

**DESCRIPTION:** The male is black with a large white spot in the centre of each wing, surrounded by a band of iridescent purplish-blue, and without the orange of the female. The pattern of the female (below) is variable, with at least six different forms in Australia.

**LIFE HISTORY:** The pale green eggs are laid singly or in clusters on the leaves of food plants such as *Asystasia* species and Paddy's Lucerne. Fully grown caterpillars are 55 mm long and dark brown or black with many long, reddish spines. When young, the caterpillars feed in groups but later live alone, feeding at night and sometimes by day. The pupa is brown, mottled with black, about 27 mm long and hangs downwards in a location away from the food plant. Females can lay more than 2500 eggs during their short lives.

**BEHAVIOUR:** Males are territorial and will defend their patch aggressively, chasing away other butterflies and even birds, mostly during the middle of the day. Courtship occurs with the male flying, making small wingbeats, just below the female. Mating lasts one or two hours.

**HABITAT:** They inhabit a variety of habitats, including savanna, open woodlands and suburban areas.

**DISTRIBUTION:** Coastal Qld, Northern NSW, north-west WA, northern NT. They also occur as vagrants over the rest of the eastern half of Australia.

**SIZE:** Male wingspan is 76 mm; female wingspan is 86 mm. Both males and females vary considerably in size.

**Below:** The wings of the female have a large, variable orange region, which is absent in the male.  **Right:** Common Eggflies mating in the position common to nymph butterflies. They may do this for several hours.

*Males are territorial and perch high in the canopy in full sunlight, patrolling for females. They also feed at puddles and on animal faeces, absorbing nutrients and minerals that are probably passed to the female during mating.*

**DESCRIPTION:** Males (above) are orange with a few black spots and streaks on the wings, without the brown and white of the female. Males are seen much more commonly than females.

**LIFE HISTORY:** The pearly-grey eggs are laid singly on the food plant, mostly on dried tendrils. Food plants are the native passion vines in the genera *Adenia*, and *Passiflora,* as well as *Hollrungia aurantioides*. The caterpillar is yellow with dark green and black bands and a number of long branched spines. It feeds singly on leaves at night.

The pupa varies from pale green to pinkish-brown, with two spectacular silver patches on the back. It has a number of large, pointed projections from the body, giving it the appearance of a dead leaf of its food plant. They fly throughout the year and are most common just after the wet season.

**BEHAVIOUR:** Adults have a strong, gliding flight and can be found flying in sunlit patches in the rainforest. Males gather together in areas of damp soil to drink the moisture produced, particularly during hot weather.

**HABITAT:** This butterfly is found only in a few small areas of coastal lowland rainforest and monsoon forest, where its food plants can be found.

**DISTRIBUTION:** Coastal Qld.

**SIZE:** Male wingspan is 75 mm; female wingspan is 82 mm.

*This species sometimes migrates around Australia in association with Australian Painted Ladies and Australian Admiral butterflies. The Meadow Argus can be found over the entire continent.*

**DESCRIPTION:** Adults are medium brown with prominent eyespots ringed with orange. The sexes are very difficult to distinguish.

**LIFE HISTORY:** The green, barrel-shaped eggs are laid singly on leaves of the food plant. Caterpillars feed on a range of native and introduced plant species in the genera *Plantago*, *Goodenia* and *Verbena*. The caterpillar grows up to 40 mm long and is black with numerous thick, branched spines. The pupa is 17 mm long, dull brown with pale blotches and hangs head-down on the food plant or on a nearby object. The time from egg to adult may take 17–62 days, depending on temperature. There are several generations per year, but females stop breeding during the dry season in tropical areas. Adults fly throughout the year in the north, and even in some of the southern parts of the range, but not during winter in Tasmania.

**BEHAVIOUR:** Adult butterflies bask in the sun on open ground, but sit with their wings folded if the temperature is too high. They may be territorial and fly rapidly within a metre of the ground, alternating one or two wingbeats with short gliding periods.

**HABITAT:** They exist in a variety of habitats, particularly woodlands, grassland and suburban areas.

**DISTRIBUTION:** Australia wide.

**SIZE:** Male wingspan is 40 mm; female wingspan is 43 mm.

*Adults of this species fly, with a jerky flight, close to the ground in sunlit patches of forest, where they feed on flowers such as Sweet Bursaria. They can be distinguished by the prominent eyespots on the wings.*

**DESCRIPTION:** The pattern of both sexes is identical, but males have a long narrow patch of grey scales near the tip of the forewing.

**LIFE HISTORY:** The pale cream-coloured eggs are laid singly or in small groups on the leaves of the food plant, which include native grasses and Kangaroo Grass. The caterpillar varies from green to brown, with dark and pale lines down the length of the body, which is covered with dense short hairs. Older caterpillars spend the day at the base of the plant or among leaf litter. The pupa is 13 mm long and green to purplish. It hangs head downwards from a leaf of the food plant. Males emerge from their pupae about three weeks before the females. There is one generation per year and adults are on the wing from October to April in Queensland and December to May in Victoria.

**BEHAVIOUR:** Females rest in cool shady areas such as gullies and creek banks during the hottest parts of the season.

**HABITAT:** They prefer wet forests, open forests and woodlands with a grassy understorey, especially damp gullies where their food plants are found. Eastern Ringed Xenica occur most commonly around the Great Dividing Range.

**DISTRIBUTION:** South-East Qld, NSW, Vic, south-east SA.

**SIZE:** Male wingspan is 39 mm; female wingspan is 44 mm.

# Blues

Family: Lycaenidae

Blues are a family of small to very small butterflies, with a few larger exceptions. Most are decorated with brilliant blues, as well as orange, violet and green. Wingspan varies between 15–53 mm. In many species there is an elongated "tail" on the hindwing that acts as a false head to direct predators away from the real head.

Species of blues have very specialised habitats and many rely on the presence of attendant ants for their survival. The family is mostly tropical, with more than 100 species living in north Queensland and fewer than ten in Tasmania.

Adults usually fly rapidly for short distances and settle on branches high in the trees. They prefer to fly in sunshine and settle when the sky is clouded over. The males of some species are territorial. There is usually a striking difference in colour between adult males and females of the same species.

The round eggs are laid on or around the food plant. The caterpillars are flattened and shaped somewhat like slaters or woodlice. Most species are associated with ants in a mutually positive relationship, but a number of species live within ant nests and feed on the larvae. Other species feed on the fruit, young leaves, buds, flowers, and seeds of a range of food plants.

This is the largest family of butterflies in Australia, making up more than one-third of the total butterfly species. There are 142 blue species in Australia and more than 6000 species worldwide.

**Top:** Blues are usually small, delicate butterflies. Most species have bluish wings but they may also be green, orange or purple.

The Common Grass-blue is one of a number of small grass-blue butterflies occurring throughout the continent. This species is the most widespread of the grass-blues and probably the most common butterfly in Australia.

**DESCRIPTION:** Adults are light blue-purple on the upperside of the wings, with a border of grey-brown that is wider in the female than the male.

**LIFE HISTORY:** Eggs are laid on the young leaves, buds, flowers and seed pods of a range of legumes, such as peas, beans, clover and lucerne. The caterpillar has a flat, light green body with a dark green line down the back and a light brown head. It is densely covered with short hairs. Caterpillars are attended by a number of ant species, including Ghost Ants, meat ants and greenhead ants, which usually benefits both partners — known as mutualism. The caterpillars rest at the base of the food plants during the day and can be very hard to find. The pupa is pinkish-brown with darker markings and is attached to the food plant. Adults are found in spring, summer and autumn. There are several generations per year.

**BEHAVIOUR:** Adults fly close to the ground among grass and weeds. They have a weak, fluttering flight and rest regularly with their wings closed.

**HABITAT:** They are found in many natural habitats, as well as parks, suburban gardens, sporting fields and pasture.

**DISTRIBUTION:** All States and Territories, but they are absent from a large area of inland WA.

**SIZE:** Male wingspan is 20 mm; female wingspan is 23 mm.

# Common Imperial Blue  *Jalmenus evagoras*

*The caterpillars of this species are attended by meat ants, which provide protection in return for a sweet substance produced by the caterpillars. This relationship, where both parties benefit, is known as mutualism.*

**DESCRIPTION:** The upperside of the wings is a pale iridescent blue with a wide black band around the edges. The hindwings have two large orange spots at the lower edge with small white bands on each side. The blue on the upperside of the wings is paler in the female than the male.

**LIFE HISTORY:** The bluish-white eggs are laid in clusters on young food plants, usually up to 2 m high, which include Weeping Mistletoe and at least 27 species of wattles. Older caterpillars are 18 mm long, varying from green to black with an orange-yellow band down each side and a black head.

When fully fed, they pupate in groups on communal webs among the leaves. There are generally three generations per year. Development from egg to pupa takes about 24 days and adults fly from October to April.

**BEHAVIOUR:** Males emerge earlier than females and congregate around the female pupae, awaiting their emergence. Adults fly within a few metres of the ground and tend to remain around the food plants, feeding on Sweet Bursaria flowers.

**HABITAT:** They prefer open forest and woodland where the food plant is present. Their populations are very localised.

**DISTRIBUTION:** South-East Qld, coastal NSW and the western half of Vic.

**SIZE:** Male wingspan is 32 mm; female wingspan is 37 mm.

**Below:** Common Imperial Blues have a small "false head" at the bottom corner of the hindwings, which is designed to distract predators from the real head.  **Right:** The caterpillars of this species pupate together in large numbers on a silken web.

# Yellow-spotted Blue *Candalides xanthospilos*

*Despite their small size, Yellow-spotted Blues are able to travel considerable distances. A single specimen was recorded in the 1800s on Lord Howe Island, 700 km off the Australian coast.*

DESCRIPTION: Both sexes are characterised by large yellow spots on the forewings. The wings of the male are mostly blue with a purple tinge, but those of the female are brown-black.

LIFE HISTORY: The egg is pale green at first then later white, laid singly on the flower buds and soft leaves of food plants, which are riceflower species. Young caterpillars feed on new shoots and hollow out grooves along the leaf surface. Older caterpillars are bright green with a yellowish line down the length of the body. They feed at night and hide during the day at the base of the food plant. The pupa is 11 mm long and brown with dark brown mottling. It is attached to the base of the food plant, among leaf litter. The caterpillar stage lasts 3–4 weeks, but the length of the pupal stage varies depending on temperature. In Queensland, adults fly from August to April, and from October to February in Victoria.

BEHAVIOUR: Adults fly close to the ground and stop regularly to rest on the ground, with their wings partly open, to bask in the sun.

HABITAT: Tall, open eucalypt forest with a heath understorey attracts this species, which prefers open areas where food plants are found.

DISTRIBUTION: Coastal Qld, NSW, Vic.

SIZE: Male wingspan is 24 mm; female wingspan is 26 mm.

*There are a number of small, blue butterfly species in Australia similar to the Wattle Blue. This species also has three different subspecies, as well as summer and winter forms.*

**DESCRIPTION:** There is significant variation in this species in different areas and at different times of the year. The upper surface of the wings is bright blue with a dark border, and the underside is brown.

**LIFE HISTORY:** The female lays pale green eggs singly on the stems or leaves of food plants, which include several species of wattle and gum tree, as well as *Sesbania* species and Whitewood. Caterpillars vary from green to yellowish-green, with a dark reddish-brown band, edged with white, down the body. They feed exposed on leaves, flowers and galls (abnormal outgrowths of plant tissue), and are attended by a range of ants, such as sugar ants and meat ants. Caterpillars are sometimes found inside the ants' nests. When fully fed, they pupate attached to the food plant. Adults fly throughout the year in Queensland but only from August to May in the south. There are several generations each year.

**BEHAVIOUR:** Males congregate on hilltops, where they set up territories and perch on shrubs and trees 3 m or more above the ground. Adults may be seen flying rapidly around food plants.

**HABITAT:** They occur over most of mainland Australia, including inland areas, and are found in dry forest, savanna woodland and arid shrublands.

**DISTRIBUTION:** Found in all States and Territories except Tasmania.

**SIZE:** Male wingspan is 22 mm; female wingspan is 21 mm.

# Purple Oak-blue  *Arhopala centaurus*

*Like many species of blue butterfly, the Purple Oak-blue sits with its wings closed when at rest, concealing it from potential predators. When active, they fly rapidly, showing flashes of brilliant blue from the topside of the wings.*

**DESCRIPTION:** Adults are a brilliant blue above the wings and pale brown with darker markings underneath. The sexes are very similar to each other.

**LIFE HISTORY:** The grey-white eggs are laid singly or in small clusters on the branches of the food plant, which also supports nests of Green Tree Ants. The caterpillar is 25 mm long and is dull green with a broad, reddish-brown band down the back, and white lines, edged with purple, down the sides. They feed exposed on young leaves and are always attended by Green Tree Ants, which protect them from predators in return for a nutritious honeydew. The pupa is 20 mm long, dull green with brown to black markings, and is attached to a single rolled leaf of the food plant. There are a number of species of food plants, including *Terminalia* species, *Corymbia* species, gum trees and tea-trees. These butterflies have several generations per year and adults occasionally migrate.

**BEHAVIOUR:** Adults often perch together in foliage, remaining settled for long periods that are interspersed with brief periods of activity.

**HABITAT:** They prefer dry forest, sand dunes, paperbark woodland and mangrove and rainforest edges, where Green Tree Ant nests are found.

**DISTRIBUTION:** There are two subspecies in Australia. *Arhopala centaurus centaurus* (above) occurs in coastal north and central Qld; the other, *Arhopala centaurus asopus* occurs in north-east WA and the northern NT.

**SIZE:** Both the male and female wingspan is 42 mm.

# Moths

No-one is sure exactly how many moth species there are in Australia, but the number is relatively high compared to other regions of the world. The best guess is between 20,000 and 30,000, which is similar to the number of flowering plant species in Australia. Probably less than half of these moth species have been named and described to science.

Moths are characterised by a number of features, but not all of them are present in all species — there are usually exceptions. They generally have two pairs of wings, but the females of some species, such as the Painted Apple Moth (*Teia anartoides*), are wingless. They generally feed using a coiled proboscis similar to butterflies, but many species, including the Hercules Moth (*Coscinocera hercules*), have no mouthparts at all. In general, moths can be distinguished from butterflies by their nocturnal activities, duller wing colours, the feathery antennae of the males, and the way they hold their wings to the sides of the body when at rest. Once again, there are exceptions to all of these rules. The most consistent difference is that the hindwings and forewings of moths are held together in flight with a system of bristles and hooks on each wing. In contrast, butterfly wings work together simply because of a strong overlap where they meet.

**Top:** Many small rainforest moths have long, narrow wings with tufts of enlarged scales along the margins. **Right:** The bodies and wings of most moths are covered with overlapping scales. **Opposite:** Many moth species found in Australia are endemic, existing nowhere else in the world. The tropics are particularly rich in colourful species.

# Case Moths
## Family: Psychidae

Case moths are a family of small to medium-sized moths that are generally dull coloured with wings that are held roof-like over the body. Wingspan varies between 10–60 mm. The family is divided into two groups — a primitive one in which both sexes are winged; and a more advanced group in which most females are wingless. Adults that are winged tend to be rapid fliers and most species are nocturnal. They can survive in diverse habitats, including suburban gardens.

The males of many species have an extendable abdomen that is used to mate with the wingless female while she is still within her case. They are often short lived, so mating takes place soon after emergence from the pupa. In some cases, the female remains within her pupal shell and the male's abdomen must penetrate this to mate with her. All adults have no mouthparts and do not feed.

The most distinctive characteristic of this family is that the caterpillars live within a silken case of their own construction. The case is lined with stems, leaves or other plant material, each one particular to that species. Upon hatching, the tiny caterpillars drift away from the mother's case on the wind, attached to short threads of silk, before constructing a case of their own. The caterpillars feed on a range of plants, keeping most of their bodies within the case while they feed.

There are more than 180 species of case moth in Australia, with about 1000 species worldwide.

**Top:** Caterpillars in this family use a range of different plant material to camouflage their cocoons. This species uses dead rolled leaves. **Right:** This case moth, seen from below, attaches long thin twigs in a spiral pattern around the body.

# Saunders' Case Moth  *Metura elongatus*

*The Saunders' Case Moth is one of the best-known insects in eastern Australia. Despite their silken protection, the caterpillars are heavily parasitised by tiny wasps, which develop inside the caterpillar and emerge a few weeks later, leaving behind a dried, empty caterpillar.*

**DESCRIPTION:** The female is wingless, with a white body and brown head. The male is strikingly patterned with black wings, a bright orange head and an orange and black banded abdomen. The caterpillar's case can reach up to 120 mm long.

**LIFE HISTORY:** The female lays eggs within her own case and the hatchling caterpillars lower themselves through the opening at the bottom of the case on threads of silk to balloon away on the wind. Each caterpillar begins to construct a small case, attaching small fragments of leaves. As the caterpillar grows, it attaches small twigs that are chewed to the right length before being sewn in. They feed on many species of gum trees, wattles, cypress, pine trees and *Cotoneaster* species. When fully fed, the mouth of the case is sewn up while the caterpillar pupates. On emergence from the pupa, the male leaves his case in search of a female. He mates with her while outside her case, reaching inside with his extendible abdomen.

**BEHAVIOUR:** They are nocturnal and males are active flyers.

**HABITAT:** Prefers open forest, parklands and suburban gardens.

**DISTRIBUTION:** Qld, NSW, Vic.

**SIZE:** Male wingspan is 30 mm; females are wingless.

**Below:** The Saunders Case Moth caterpillar is strikingly coloured but rarely seen. It seldom ventures far from the opening.  **Right:** This case moth is a common sight on fences and branches during summer.

# Ghost Moths

### Family: Hepialidae

Ghost moths are a family of small to very large, often beautifully patterned moths that rest with their wings held roof-like over the body. Wingspan varies between 20–250 mm. Most species are brown or grey, but may include shades of green, blue and pink.

They are found in a range of habitats, but particularly open forests. Adults are mostly on the wing in autumn, following the autumn rains. On wet nights, hundreds of flying moths may be seen, but all may be gone by the next day. They can be strong fliers and are often attracted to lights at night.

Adult ghost moths are generally short lived, so mating takes place soon after emergence. The females of some species are capable of laying tens of thousands of eggs, which are usually scattered randomly over the ground and have a very low survival rate.

Caterpillars generally feed in concealed situations, such as within the soil or inside tree trunks, consuming roots or boring into living wood. A number of species feed on leaf litter or the bases of grass tussocks. The adults often leave behind an empty pupal case protruding from a hole in the soil or trunk. The adults of most species live only a couple of days and have no mouthparts, so do not eat or drink.

There are about 120 ghost moth species in Australia, which is more than one-fifth of the known species in the world.

**Left:** Females produce hundreds of eggs throughout their lives, broadcasting them as she flies at night.

Foresters are a family of mostly small moths that are often brilliantly coloured. Some species are black or metallic blue, others are green or orange or have wasp-like markings. At rest, adults sit with the wings loosely folded over the abdomen and the antennae extended out in front of the head. Wingspan varies between 12–24 mm.

There are three subfamilies within this family, but only one occurs in Australia and most of these species are particularly small. They are found in a range of habitats and are especially common in rainforests. Adults defend themselves from predators by using powerful chemicals, such as cyanide.

Unlike most moth species, foresters are mostly active during the day, when they can often be seen feeding at flowers. Some species are also attracted to lights at night. Mating takes place soon after emergence from the pupa and the eggs are laid in groups either on or near the food plants.

The caterpillars are thick-bodied and hairy but rarely seen. They feed on the leaves of a wide range of food plants at night, particularly native grapes, either chewing the entire leaf or, more commonly, scraping away the upper surface of the leaf. The caterpillars hide among the dead leaves of the food plant or in leaf litter during the day. They leave the food plant to construct a cocoon in a sheltered location elsewhere.

Only 43 species are known in Australia, from a world population of more than 1000.

**Top:** Forester moths include some of the most spectacularly coloured species in Australia.

# Cup Moths
## Family: Limacodidae

This family is best known for its colourful caterpillars, many of which possess stinging hairs. Not all species are capable of stinging, but the caterpillars are generally flattened, slug-like and brightly coloured. Adult moths are stout-bodied and dull-coloured, usually brown, orange or grey. Wingspan varies between 15–75 mm. They are found in a range of habitats, particularly open forests and rainforests.

The family's common name derives from these moth's cup-shaped cocoons, which are usually attached to twigs and are extremely tough. Adults are generally nocturnal and fly rapidly and haphazardly. The males in particular may be attracted to lights at night. A few rainforest species are active during the day.

Adults do not possess mouthparts and are generally short lived. Mating takes place soon after emergence from the pupa. The females of some species cover the egg mass with scales from their bodies, helping protect the eggs from parasites.

Caterpillars tend to feed openly on the foliage during the day, particularly those species protected by stinging hairs. They feed on a range of food plants, including many species of gum trees. Some species can defoliate small gum trees when present in large numbers. A high proportion of caterpillars are attacked by a range of parasitic wasps. To emerge from the pupa, the adult pushes off the cap, leaving behind the characteristic empty cup-shaped pupa.

About 70 cup moth species of are known from Australia, from a world total of more than 1000 species.

**Top:** Some species of cup moths resemble Chinese boats (called Junks). This is sometimes used as an alternative common name. **Right:** Reds, greens and greys are common colours on cup moth caterpillars. The patterns are sometimes extremely intricate.

# Mottled Cup Moth    *Doratifera vulnerans*

*The caterpillars of this species are known for the painful welts they inflict if they are touched. The presence of histamines in the venom can cause some people to have severe allergic reactions on contact with this caterpillar.*

**DESCRIPTION:** In contrast to the brightly coloured caterpillars, the adult moths (top) are a drab red-brown and grey, with a fat body covered in fine scales.

**LIFE HISTORY:** The eggs are laid in batches on the leaves of the food plant and covered with scales from the female's body. Young caterpillars mass together and feed on the surface tissue of the leaves, so that only a skeleton remains. They eat the foliage of gum trees and paperbarks, but will also eat ornamental plants and fruit trees, especially apricots. When fully fed, the caterpillars spin a tough, 12 mm long, cup-shaped cocoon, in which they pupate. Two pairs of rosettes adorn their backs, each composed of many hollow spines that do not actually penetrate human skin; instead, the tips are ruptured on contact and a toxin that causes a rash is released.

**BEHAVIOUR:** The adults fly at night and settle during the day on foliage. They are rarely seen.

**HABITAT:** These moths are found in dry eucalypt forest and suburban areas. They can be common in gardens and parks with young stands of gum trees.

**DISTRIBUTION:** NSW, ACT, Vic, SA.

**SIZE:** Male wingspan is 25 mm; female wingspan is 30 mm; both may vary in size.

**Top:** A Mottled Cup Moth caterpillar with the stinging rosettes retracted whilst the caterpillar feeds. **Below:** Adult cup moths are drab and hardly ever seen, unlike their more colourful offspring.

# Loopers

## Family: Geometridae

Loopers are a family of small to large moths with broad, generally triangular wings that are held flat at the sides of the body. The wings are usually patterned with intricate lines and zig-zags, which help camouflage the adult against its background. The geometric shape of the wings gives the family its scientific name. Wingspan varies between 12–120 mm.

Loopers are found in numerous habitats, from rainforest to open forest and from grasslands to suburban areas. Adult moths are mostly nocturnal and are designed to be well camouflaged during the day.

Mating takes place soon after emergence from the pupa. The eggs tend to be slightly flattened and are laid singly or in groups, sometimes piled in heaps on top of each other, around the food plants.

The family's common name, loopers, arose because the caterpillars do not have legs in the middle of the body, causing them to move by extending the front half of the body out and looping the back half forwards. In most species, the caterpillar is long and slender, often with a range of tubercles or projections spiking upwards from the body.

The caterpillars generally feed openly on the leaves of many food plants and often closely resemble the leaves or twigs of their host. They tend to feed on larger plants, high up in the canopy, but, despite their abundance, very rarely become pests.

This is a particularly large family, with 1300 Australian species and more than 21,000 species worldwide.

**Left, top to bottom:** The Twin Emerald Moth (*Chlorocoma dichlorama*) demonstrates how most looper moths sit with their wings pressed against a flat surface; Looper caterpillars have no legs in the middle of the body, so they move in a continuous looping fashion.

# Four O' Clock Moth  *Dysphania fenestrata*

*Unlike many moths, both the adults and caterpillars of this species are brightly coloured. The caterpillars sit upright on branches of the food plant and, at first glance, look like flowers, giving them superb camouflage.*

**DESCRIPTION:** The wings are dark purplish-black with pale blue-white translucent patches. There are sometimes small yellow patches near the base of the forewings. The abdomen is yellow with black bands.

**LIFE HISTORY:** The female lays eggs on leaves of rainforest trees in the genus *Carallia*. Young caterpillars are greenish, becoming bright yellow as they grow, although older greenish-yellow caterpillars occur in some areas. Caterpillars are medium-sized and conspicuous, with rows of black eyespots along the body. They sit upright on the plant when not feeding and have no legs in the middle of the body, meaning they move in a looping fashion. Tiny parasitic wasps lay their white eggs on the outside of the caterpillar's body, usually just behind the head. When fully fed, the caterpillars pupate between leaves tied together with silk.

**BEHAVIOUR:** As its common name suggests, this species flies in the late afternoon (around four o'clock), as well as in the early morning. They tend to rest on foliage during the day. They are strong fliers, often remaining in flight for considerable periods.

**HABITAT:** Four O'Clock Moths inhabit a range of rainforest types, as well as suburban areas.

**DISTRIBUTION:** Coastal Qld from Cape York to Yeppoon, northern WA, NT.

**SIZE:** Both the male and female wingspan is 80–85 mm.

**Top:** The caterpillars of this species are host to a number of parasites. The eggs of a parasitic wasp can be seen just behind the caterpillar's head. **Below:** Four O'Clock Moths are most active in the late afternoon and early morning. They can also be seen flying through the rainforest at night.

*This species can be a serious pest in gum plantations, particularly in Tasmania. Unlike the many moth species that are active during summer, to avoid the heat the Autumn Gum Moth spends summer underground, as a pupa, and emerges when the temperature drops and the rains begin.*

**DESCRIPTION:** Adults have mottled grey and brown forewings with pale orange hindwings that are partly visible when at rest.

**LIFE HISTORY:** The female lays eggs on young leaves of blue gum, messmate, yellow gum and related species. The caterpillars grow up to 40 mm long. Older caterpillars are bluish-green with red markings and two large yellow spots about halfway down the body. They hide during the day in groups within a shelter made by curling one or more leaves over and sewing them together with silk. These shelters can often be found at the end of branches that have had all leaves stripped from them. They leave the shelter at night to feed. If disturbed, the caterpillars regurgitate a sticky green fluid. Young caterpillars (above) tend to skeletonise the leaves by scraping off the surface of the leaf, avoiding the veins, but older individuals eat the entire leaf. Caterpillars occur during winter and spring.

**BEHAVIOUR:** Both sexes fly at night, and sometimes during the day, throughout autumn and early winter.

**HABITAT:** Found in dry forest and gum plantations, as well as in roadside and suburban parks and gardens.

**DISTRIBUTION:** Southern Qld, NSW, Vic, Tas, SA.

**SIZE:** Both the male and female wingspan is up to 45 mm.

The Grevillea Looper bears a remarkable resemblance to a dead gum leaf, although this is not one of its food plants. The background colour of the wings exactly matches that of a dead leaf, with a pale yellow "midvein" stretching between the outspread wings.

**DESCRIPTION:** The colour of the wings is variable, generally reddish-brown or pink through to yellowish-grey, but always resembles a dead gum leaf.

**LIFE HISTORY:** The female lays her eggs on the leaves of small to medium-sized shrubs of *Grevillea, Hakea* and *Banksia* species. Caterpillars can be found during summer and autumn and grow to 55 mm. They are hairless and fleshy, and range in colour from purplish-red to greenish-brown, with small white dots all over the body and a black stripe down the back. They feed at night and rest during the day on foliage. If disturbed, a caterpillar will rear up and tuck its head under its body. When fully fed, the caterpillar constructs a loose silken cocoon among leaf litter.

**BEHAVIOUR:** Grevillea Loopers are nocturnal. Adults are strong fliers that are on the wing during autumn and spring in some areas, or for most of the year in others.

**HABITAT:** They prefer dry forest that has an understorey of *Grevillea, Hakea* or *Banksia* species. They are also common in suburban areas.

**DISTRIBUTION:** This moth occurs over most of Australia.

**SIZE:** Male wingspan is 55 mm; female wingspan is up to 60 mm.

# Bizarre Looper  *Eucyclodes pieroides*

*Because of their habit of feeding on avocados and guava, Bizarre Looper caterpillars have been identified by the New Zealand quarantine service as a potential threat in imports from Australia.*

DESCRIPTION: The adult male's body is mottled grey and white, and the wings have wide, irregular bands of white and pale grey, with the grey bands being suffused with white dots. The female's wings are mid-green with an irregular pale brown edge with darker brown spots; her body is also pale brown. The wings are serrated at the edges.

LIFE HISTORY: The oval, flattened eggs are laid on the leaves of food plants, which include a range of gum tree species, wattles, *Terminalia* species and the introduced Giant Sensitive Plant, guava, cherry, avocado and rose. They also feed on the flowers of mango trees. The young caterpillar has no flanges but covers its body with its own droppings (frass). After the second moult, large flanges develop and make the caterpillars resemble dead or damaged leaves. Caterpillars are attacked by fly parasites from the family Tachinidae. When fully fed, the caterpillar builds a silken cocoon and pupates among leaf litter, emerging after about two weeks.

BEHAVIOUR: They are nocturnal. Adults are active at night and rest by day with their wings pressed against a leaf or tree trunk.

HABITAT: Found in dry forest and horticultural and suburban areas.

DISTRIBUTION: From Cooktown in Qld to Port Macquarie in NSW. Also found in NT.

SIZE: Adult wingspan is 27 mm.

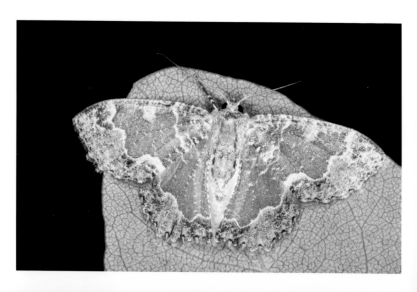

*This species belongs to a group of spectacular day-flying moths from New Guinea, Borneo and other parts of South-East Asia. There are at least ten other Milionia species in Borneo alone. Unlike these species, however, the Australian species is active only at night.*

**DESCRIPTION:** The base colour of the forewings varies from blue-black to dull brown with a diagonal yellow band and an inner margin of red. The hindwings are dark brown with a yellow spot in the centre that varies in size and shape. There are also yellow marks around the scalloped edges of the hindwings. ˙

**LIFE HISTORY:** The caterpillars and food plants are not known from Australia. The caterpillars of overseas species are bluish-black with a prominent orange head and white lines down the body.

Like all looper caterpillars, they do not possess legs along the middle of the body. When they have finished feeding, the caterpillars drop to the ground on a silken thread and pupate about 5 cm under the soil surface. Other species are known to feed on conifers.

**BEHAVIOUR:** Boarmid Moths are nocturnal and the adults are attracted to lights at night. In closely related overseas species, both males and females feed on nectar and males also absorb moisture from cattle dung, dead animals and damp mud, possibly to obtain scarce minerals.

**HABITAT:** Found in rainforest.

**DISTRIBUTION:** From Cooktown to Innisfail in Queensland.

**SIZE:** Adult wingspan is 55 mm.

# Anthelid Moths

## Family: Anthelidae

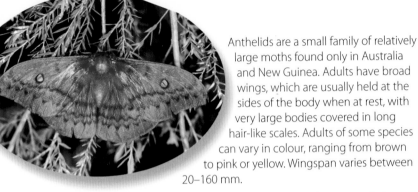

Anthelids are a small family of relatively large moths found only in Australia and New Guinea. Adults have broad wings, which are usually held at the sides of the body when at rest, with very large bodies covered in long hair-like scales. Adults of some species can vary in colour, ranging from brown to pink or yellow. Wingspan varies between 20–160 mm.

The family is generally nocturnal and while males frequently come to lights at night, females rarely do. They are found in a range of habitats, but particularly in open forests where the food plants of the caterpillars are most abundant. Most adults have no mouthparts and do not feed.

The female emerges from the pupa fully laden with eggs and mates almost immediately. She lays eggs singly or in groups around the food plant. The caterpillars are covered with hair, ranging from a full covering of long filaments to bundles of short, sharp spikes. These spikes may cause an allergic reaction in some humans.

The caterpillars feed exposed on the food plants at night and hide during the day. They eat a range of food plants, particularly gum trees, wattles and grasses. The caterpillars always seek a sheltered location to pupate and may push their hairs through the double walls of the cocoon as ongoing protection.

There are 74 species of anthelid moth in Australia and at least twelve species in New Guinea.

**Top:** Many anthelid moth species are large and their bodies are characteristically covered with long, hair-like scales. **Left:** Anthelid moths sit with their wings out to the sides of the body. The wings also tend to be broad and pointed at the tips.

*This species is also known as the Prickly Gum Moth, due to the sharp spines all over the caterpillars' bodies (above). These spines are broken off and pushed through the wall of the cocoon when the caterpillar pupates, further protecting it from predators.*

**DESCRIPTION:** The wings are patterned with grey and brown. The male is smaller than the female and has more contrasting markings.

**LIFE HISTORY:** Eggs are laid on the leaves of food plants, which include numerous gum tree species. Caterpillars feed throughout spring and summer and grow to 110 mm long. If these caterpillars are handled, spines on their skin can break off and penetrate a person's skin. These spines can be painful and must be individually pulled out or they will produce skin irritation and swelling. In severe cases, anaphylactic shock may even result. When fully fed, the caterpillars often leave the food plant to pupate and may cross suburban gardens or streets. The caterpillar chooses a sheltered location to spin a pale, cream-brown bag-like cocoon.

**BEHAVIOUR:** These moths are nocturnal. Males are strong fliers that frequently come to lights at night, although females rarely do. When disturbed, the male rears up its body to expose the white underside and extends its legs, making it resemble a striking spider. Adults do not feed and live for just two to three days. They are on the wing during April and May.

**HABITAT:** They are found in open forest and suburban areas.

**DISTRIBUTION:** They are distributed from the Carnarvon Range in Qld, through to the coast and tablelands of NSW and most of Vic.

**SIZE:** Male wingspan is 150 mm; female wingspan is 160 mm.

# Snout Moths
## Family: Lasiocampidae

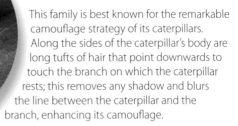

This family is best known for the remarkable camouflage strategy of its caterpillars. Along the sides of the caterpillar's body are long tufts of hair that point downwards to touch the branch on which the caterpillar rests; this removes any shadow and blurs the line between the caterpillar and the branch, enhancing its camouflage.

Adults are medium to large, "furry" moths and many species have a long "snout" at the front of the head. Wingspan varies between 20–170 mm. They are found in a range of habitats, but particularly prefer open forests.

Most species are nocturnal and males regularly come to lights at night. In some species, the males fly during the day and the females at night. Although the males have eyes that are adapted to night-flying, rather than day-flying, they are able to use pheromones emitted by the females to locate mates during the day. Adults usually have no mouthparts at all and do not feed.

The female emerges from the pupa fully laden with eggs in her enlarged abdomen. She mates immediately, if possible, to fertilise these eggs and lays them singly or in groups on the food plants. The caterpillars feed alone on the leaves of food plants, which comprise a range of woody trees and shrubs. The caterpillars of most species feed at night. Pupation generally occurs in a tough, silken cocoon hidden in leaf litter or under bark.

There are about 70 snout moth species in Australia and more than 1500 species worldwide.

**Top:** Snout moths are named after the long, snout-like projection at the front of the head in some species. **Left:** Snout moth caterpillars are perfectly designed to blend in with the branches of the food plant.

# Prominents

Family: Notodontidae

## Lobster Moth  *Neostauropus habrochlora*

*The Lobster Moth caterpillar (below) has a truly remarkable arrangement of legs. The first pair of true legs are short and claw-like, while the next two pairs are extremely long, perhaps the longest of any caterpillar. The back legs are modified into a pair of elongated, slender filaments.*

**DESCRIPTION:** Adults are a dull mossy green, with intricate patterns of brown and grey on the forewings, which gives them excellent camouflage on lichen-covered tree trunks. The wings are folded flat alongside the body when at rest, with the forewings covering all but a narrow strip of the hindwings.

**LIFE HISTORY:** The egg and food plants are not known. The caterpillars of this species are characterised by the odd arrangement of legs and by spines that run down the back of the body. The rear three body segments are also expanded and curl back towards the front. The reason for this arrangement is not known. There is some suggestion that the elongated legs may be used to detect chemicals or other aspects of the environment. A sharp spike on the pupa's head is used by the emerging moth to cut its way out of the very tough silken cocoon.

**BEHAVIOUR:** They are nocturnal and adults readily come to lights at night. Nothing else is known of the behaviour of this species.

**HABITAT:** Found in rainforest.

**DISTRIBUTION:** North Queensland, from Cape York to Bundaberg.

**SIZE:** Adult wingspan is 35 mm.

# Emperor Moths
### Family: Saturniidae

Emperor moths belong to a family of very large moths mostly found in the tropics and subtropics of the world. The head and body are covered with long, hair-like scales and the size of the body (though large) is small in comparison to the wings. The wings are held out to the sides when at rest and may be beautifully patterned, particularly with eyespots. Wingspan varies between 65–275 mm. This family includes the largest moths in Australia and the largest in the world.

Most species are nocturnal and the males frequently come to lights at night. They may be strong, bat-like fliers. Emperor moths are found mostly in open forests and rainforests.

Mating takes place soon after emergence, and most species do not feed as adults. Males may be attracted to pheromones produced by the females, which can be detected from several kilometres away.

The caterpillars are large and fleshy, often with colourful spikes (scoli) along the body. They feed alone on the leaves of food plants, which include both native and introduced species. Caterpillars often feed exposed on branches during the day, and numerous caterpillars of some species are killed as a result of attacks by parasitic wasps. When a caterpillar is finished feeding, it spins a very tough, silken cocoon, in which it may remain for several years. The cocoon is constructed on tree trunks or in foliage and may incorporate leaves or fragments of bark.

Australia is poorly represented when it comes to emperor moth species, with only fifteen species present here out of 1500 species worldwide.

**Top:** Emperor moths are characterised by fat, furry bodies, particularly the females. **Left:** Most species have eyespots on their wings, although in some these are very small.

*Both the adults and caterpillars of this species are the largest insects most Australians ever see. They are very common across southern Australia but their populations vary dramatically from year to year.*

**DESCRIPTION:** The colour of the wings varies from dark yellow to red-brown. Males are slimmer than females and have very large antennae.

**LIFE HISTORY:** The female lays several dozen yellow, broadly oval eggs in rows on the leaves of food plants. Newly hatched caterpillars are black for the first week or so after hatching; older caterpillars are light green and are surprisingly well camouflaged among the foliage, with a yellow stripe down each side and small, blue-tipped red spikes (scoli) all over the body. They can reach 130 mm in length. When fully fed, the caterpillars become pale purple and wander in search of somewhere to pupate. They spin a tough, brown, oval-shaped cocoon. Pupation may take as little as 40 days or as much as ten years. Caterpillars feed on a number of gum tree species and introduced plants such as Peppercorn.

**BEHAVIOUR:** The moths are large and bat-like, active at night and frequently attracted to lights. The adults do not feed and are relatively short lived. The flying period of the adults is restricted to spring and summer through most of their range.

**HABITAT:** Found in wet and dry forest, woodland (particularly eucalypt woodland) and suburban areas.

**DISTRIBUTION:** Qld, NSW, ACT, Vic.

**SIZE:** Male wingspan is 120 mm; female wingspan is 125 mm.

*This species is similar to, but much less common than, the Emperor Gum Moth. The adults are almost identical but the caterpillars are very different, this species lacking most of the red and blue spikes (scoli) of its more abundant relative.*

**DESCRIPTION:** The females are slightly larger than the males, which have large feathery antennae. The adult is very similar to the Emperor Gum Moth but is much more orange, with pink eyespots on the forewings and orange ones on the hindwings.

**LIFE HISTORY:** The female lays eggs on the young foliage of gum trees and the caterpillars feed openly during the day. Caterpillars are also known to feed on birch. Young caterpillars are pale brown with white lines along the top and sides and small yellow spots and scoli. There are also seven black, raised tubercles ringed with red. The caterpillar grows to 85 mm and, when older, the body is covered with short white bristles. It has a thick white-pink stripe down the side of the body from just behind the head to the rear end. The pupa is brown and oval, made of very tough silk and attached to bark or a branch.

**BEHAVIOUR:** They are nocturnal. Young caterpillars curl the head under the body when threatened, exposing the scoli on the thorax. Adults fly during spring, summer and autumn.

**HABITAT:** Found in open forest and some suburban areas.

**DISTRIBUTION:** South-East Qld, NSW, ACT, Vic, Tas, SA and south-east WA.

**SIZE:** The adult wingspan is 120–140 mm.

# Hercules Moth · *Coscinocera hercules*

*This is the largest and most spectacular moth in Australia. It may also have the largest wing area of any moth or butterfly in the world. The caterpillars are also bigger than those of any other moth or butterfly species in Australia, growing up to 145 mm long.*

DESCRIPTION: The female (below) is larger and paler than the male. The male also has a long "tail" at the end of each hindwing and a pair of large, feathery antennae.

LIFE HISTORY: The female lays about 230 brown disc-shaped eggs, either singly or in small groups. Upon hatching, the caterpillar is covered in a thick coating of white wax, which it loses after moulting twice more. Older caterpillars are pale blue-green with a series of bright yellow spine-like structures down the length of the body. The caterpillar spins a large cocoon of very tough silk among foliage and pupation takes several weeks. The caterpillars feed on a range of plants including the Cheese Tree and Queensland Poplar.

BEHAVIOUR: Males are active fliers and their wings quickly become worn and tattered. They are often attracted to lights at night. Females are generally inactive and sometimes remain on the outside of the cocoon for their entire lives, awaiting a passing male. Adults fly most of the year but are more common from January to April.

HABITAT: Hercules Moths are found in a range of rainforest types.

DISTRIBUTION: Iron Range to Mackay in north Queensland.

SIZE: Male wingspan is 260 mm; female wingspan is 280 mm.

# Hawk Moths

## Family: Sphingidae

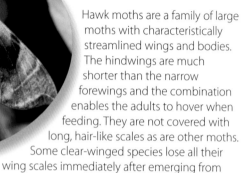

Hawk moths are a family of large moths with characteristically streamlined wings and bodies. The hindwings are much shorter than the narrow forewings and the combination enables the adults to hover when feeding. They are not covered with long, hair-like scales as are other moths. Some clear-winged species lose all their wing scales immediately after emerging from the pupa. The wingspans of hawk moths vary between 35–190 mm.

Most species are nocturnal, but they can often be seen flying at dusk or even earlier. They are excellent fliers and are able to reach the nectar in deep-throated flowers, which makes many species important pollinators. Most species live in tropical or subtropical forests, but some are found in many habitats across Australia.

Adults are long lived and mate end to end. The eggs are flat and usually pale green. They are laid singly in carefully chosen locations on the leaves of food plants. The caterpillars are generally large and fleshy, with eyespots or other patterns, and almost always have a large spike at the end of the abdomen (called the dorsal horn). Caterpillars feed exposed on the leaves of food plants during the day, particularly on plants within the grape, gardenia and morning glory families. Caterpillars pupate in the soil and leaf litter and do not construct a cocoon.

There are about 60 hawk moth species in Australia and more than 1200 species worldwide.

**Top:** The forewings and thorax of the Peaceful Hawk Moth are patterned with dark brown and lighter brown swirls in a combination characteristic of this species.

# Vine Hawk Moth *Theretra oldenlandiae*

*The Vine Hawk Moth caterpillar feeds on numerous plant species within eight different plant families. Its adaptability to so many food plants has enabled it to thrive from India and Sri Lanka through much of Asia to Australia.*

DESCRIPTION: The forewings have a thick cream band bordered by bands of dark brown. The hindwings are a light fawn colour, similar to the body. A pinkish stripe runs the length of the body to the tip of the abdomen. The sexes look very similar to each other.

LIFE HISTORY: The female lays eggs singly on a range of food plants, including native grape, willow herb, cocky apple, guinea flower, elephant ear, and the introduced Grape Vine, Egyptian Star Cluster, fuschias, garlands, Argentine Trumpet Vine, balsam and Arum Lily. Because it will feed on introduced and ornamental grape vines, it can sometimes be a minor pest but the damage is minimal. The caterpillar is black with pale markings and pairs of orange eyespots on each segment of the body. At the rear end is a thin, straight spike (dorsal horn) that is waved about as the caterpillar moves.

BEHAVIOUR: They are nocturnal. Adults can be seen flying at dusk or hovering around while feeding on deep-throated flowers.

HABITAT: Found in a range of habitats, from rainforests to suburban areas.

DISTRIBUTION: Eastern Qld, coastal NSW, north-west WA and NT.

SIZE: The adult wingspan is 60 mm.

# Processionary Moths
## Family: Thaumetopoeidae

## Sparshalli Moth  *Trichiocercus sparshalli*

*Adult Sparshalli Moths use "thanatosis", or feigning death, as a defence against predators. The moth will fall to the ground and lie upside down when disturbed, pretending to be dead. The abdomen is curled up and the long scales at the tip of the abdomen are splayed outwards.*

**DESCRIPTION:** The caterpillar (above) is covered with long white hairs, with a red stripe down the back and black triangular markings. Adults are white to light grey, covered with very long fluffy scales, and with a short proboscis. They sometimes have a red bald patch on the back of the thorax, just behind the head. Males have an additional tuft of long scales at the end of the abdomen.

**LIFE HISTORY:** The eggs are deposited in a single layer on the leaves of the food plant and are covered with special scales that are shed from the end of the female's abdomen. The eggs are dome-shaped with a broad, flattened base. Caterpillars feed on gum leaves at night and shelter under loose bark on the trunk during the day. Young caterpillars feed in groups and will follow each other around in a procession. They grow to 40 mm. Food plants include gums such as Red Box and Silver-Leaved Stringybark.

**BEHAVIOUR:** Males fly to lights at night but females rarely do. Adults fly during spring, summer and autumn.

**HABITAT:** Found in dry forest and suburban parks.

**DISTRIBUTION:** Qld, NSW, SA, South-West WA, NT.

**SIZE:** The adult wingspan is 40–50 mm.

# Tussock Moths
Family: Lymantriidae

## Painted Apple Moth  *Teia anartoides*

*The female Painted Apple Moth is wingless and, after emerging from the pupa, produces a powerful pheromone that attracts males from considerable distances away.*

**DESCRIPTION:** The female has a large, brown, furry abdomen and she does not move away from the cocoon after emergence. The male has dark brown forewings mottled with black and white markings, with bright orange and black hindwings.

**LIFE HISTORY:** After mating, the female lays several hundred white eggs on the outside of the cocoon and dies soon after. The caterpillars disperse from the eggs by drifting on the wind, with the help of a long thread of silk. They feed on wattles, birch, apple trees and *Grevillea* species, growing to 50 mm. The orange-brown caterpillars feed alone out in the open during the day. There are characteristically four large white-grey tufts of long hair on the back (below). These hairs, which give the family tussock moths their name, may irritate the skin of some people. Caterpillars pupate among leaves in a cocoon, into which the caterpillar's body hairs are woven for protection. The caterpillars can be found throughout the year but are most common during winter.

**BEHAVIOUR:** The male is a reasonably strong flier at night and is on the wing during spring, summer and autumn.

**HABITAT:** Found in open forest, suburban areas and horticultural areas such as orchards, where it can be a minor pest.

**DISTRIBUTION:** Qld, NSW, ACT, Vic, Tas, SA.

**SIZE:** Male wingspan is up to 30 mm; female is wingless.

# Tiger Moths
## Family: Arctiidae

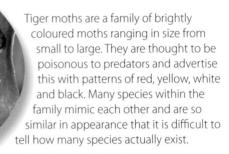

Tiger moths are a family of brightly coloured moths ranging in size from small to large. They are thought to be poisonous to predators and advertise this with patterns of red, yellow, white and black. Many species within the family mimic each other and are so similar in appearance that it is difficult to tell how many species actually exist.

A number of species have hearing organs on the thorax to listen for the presence of bats at night. They are also able to produce sounds beyond our hearing, as a warning to bats that they are poisonous. Wingspan varies between 10–85 mm.

Adults are generally nocturnal, but one of the four Australian subfamilies has members that fly during the day. They are generally not strong fliers. Tiger moths are found in a range of habitats across Australia.

Mating takes place end to end and the dome-shaped, flat-bottomed eggs are laid singly or in batches on food plants. The caterpillars feed on a diverse range of food plants, including lichens, many of which are poisonous. Because the caterpillars are protected by poisons, they may feed in exposed locations during the day. When young, the caterpillars remain in groups but move out to live solitary lives as they grow. They are hairy, but generally not colourfully patterned, and pupate among leaves or under bark or leaf litter in a flimsy cocoon.

There are about 280 species of tiger moth in Australia and more than 6000 species worldwide.

**Top:** *Amata* spp. moths mating. The genus *Amata* includes dozens of species, but very little is known of their biology. **Right, top to bottom:** The Red-headed Amerila (*Amerila rubripes*) also produces toxins to deter predators. The toxins probably come from its food plants; Tiger moths are usually poisonous to predators and advertise this with contrasting colours.

This species is a member of a subfamily of tiger moths called Lithosiinae (or footmen), which contains about 200 species that feed on lichens, mosses or algae. The Blue & Yellow Tiger Moth also occurs in South-East Asia and on Pacific islands.

DESCRIPTION: The forewings are brightly patterned with pale yellow and metallic blue. The body is slender, and both the forewings and hindwings are relatively narrow but broadly rounded at the ends. The hindwings are pale yellow without any pattern and the abdomen is the same darker yellow as the forewings.

LIFE HISTORY: Very little is known of this moth's life history, but the caterpillars probably feed on lichens, mosses and algae on tree trunks. They pupate in a flimsy silken cocoon.

BEHAVIOUR: Blue & Yellow Tiger Moths are nocturnal. The adults are active at night and are attracted to lights, but are not strong fliers. They rest during the day with their wings folded over and down the sides of the body. Adult moths possess warning colours and are probably poisonous if eaten by vertebrate predators, particularly bats. The moths have hearing organs and sound-producing organs on the sides of the thorax; these may be used to warn nearby bats that the moth is poisonous, or to jam the bat's echolocation system.

HABITAT: Found in rainforest.

DISTRIBUTION: They are found in north Queensland, south to Mackay.

SIZE: The adult wingspan is 35 mm.

# Magpie Moth  *Nyctemera amica*

*Magpie Moth caterpillars use poisons from their preferred food plants (*Senecio *species) for their own defence. Research has found the poisons persisting in the bodies of the adults, as well as the eggs, and even in the bodies of the tiny wasps that parasitise the caterpillars.*

**DESCRIPTION:** Adults have dark brown-black wings with white to creamish markings. The abdomen is banded orange and black, suggesting it is poisonous.

**LIFE HISTORY:** The female lays groups of whitish eggs on the leaves of the food plants. After hatching, the caterpillars feed on *Senecio* species, both native and introduced, from September to March. Fully grown caterpillars are black, covered with long bristles, and have red stripes down the back of the body and sides.

They pupate in a flimsy cocoon that incorporates some of the caterpillar's bristles. Pupation takes two to six weeks.

**BEHAVIOUR:** They are day-flying, as well as nocturnal. In some years, the adults may undertake migratory flights when the local population gets too high, but where they are flying to and from is unknown. They may also be important in pollinating some flowering shrubs, such as the lilly pilly. Adults fly most months through the year but particularly from October to May.

**HABITAT:** They occupy a number of habitats, but most commonly open pasture and grasslands.

**DISTRIBUTION:** Central and southern Qld, NSW, Vic, Tas, SA, South-West WA.

**SIZE:** Male wingspan is 45 mm; female wingspan is 35–40 mm.

*This species is very colourful. Because it flies both day and night, it is often mistaken for a butterfly.*

**DESCRIPTION:** The forewings of the adults are speckled with red and black, and the hindwings are pale blue with black markings.

**LIFE HISTORY:** The female lays eggs on the leaves of food plants, which include forget-me-nots, Paterson's Curse and Common Heliotrope. The caterpillar grows to 25 mm and is black with broken cream-coloured lines along the body and long grey hairs in small groups. The head is dark red. They feed openly on plants during the day and pupate in a loosely woven cocoon in the soil or at the base of the food plant. The caterpillars absorb a range of poisonous chemicals from their food plants and use them for their own defence. These chemicals may also be incorporated into the pheromones used to attract females for mating. Caterpillars are found in summer and autumn.

**BEHAVIOUR:** They are day-flying, as well as nocturnal. When disturbed, the adults may fall to the ground, feigning death. They may also bleed from the thorax (called reflex bleeding) to deter predators. Adults fly from September to May, with peaks in January and April.

**HABITAT:** Prefer agricultural areas, roadsides and suburban parks and gardens. They are particularly common in abandoned weedy blocks in suburban areas.

**DISTRIBUTION:** Found over most of Australia, in all States and Territories.

**SIZE:** The adult wingspan is 30-35 mm.

*Like many species in the tiger moth family, the Red-headed Amerila is toxic to predators. It produces a number of chemicals (including cyanide) which the caterpillars probably absorb from food plants.*

**DESCRIPTION:** The sexes appear very similar to each other. The forewings are pure white with patches of clear membrane at the trailing edges. The hindwings are also white, but are much smaller. The thorax and bases of the forewings are white with a series of black spots, but may become a dirty cream-yellow as the moth ages, particularly if a great quantity of froth has been produced from the thorax over time. Running across the thorax is a red to crimson stripe, which is variable in width. The bases of the legs are also crimson.

**LIFE HISTORY:** The caterpillars have been found feeding on the native vine *Gymnanthera nitida* and the introduced Rubber Vine. Nothing else is known of their life history.

**BEHAVIOUR:** They are nocturnal and the adults are attracted to lights at night. Adults produce a frothy white to orange fluid from glands on the thorax when disturbed. Because the food plants are toxic, this substance is thought to be poisonous to vertebrate predators and acts as a deterrent to bats (at night) or to mammals and birds (by day) that may encounter these moths.

**HABITAT:** Found in rainforest.

**DISTRIBUTION:** Occurs from the Kimberley in WA, across the Top End of NT and in Queensland, ranging south to Yeppoon.

**SIZE:** The adult wingspan is 60 mm.

*This remarkable species employs a number of defensive strategies against predators. It produces bubbles of froth containing toxic chemicals such as acetylcholine, carotenoids and pyrazines.*

**DESCRIPTION:** The forewings are medium to dark brown, with clear patches of membrane towards the outer edges. The thorax and the bases of the forewings are pure white with black spots. Hindwings are a dirty cream colour with a similar brown pattern as the forewings. The abdomen is the same light crimson as the legs. There are five members of this genus in Australia, but Croker's Moth is the most widespread.

**LIFE HISTORY:** Nothing is known of the life history of this species.

**BEHAVIOUR:** They are nocturnal and adults are attracted to lights at night. When disturbed, the adult moth produces a bubbly orange froth from glands on its thorax (below) and simultaneously makes a loud sizzling sound. The food plants of the caterpillars are not known, but because related overseas species feed on plants that contain heart poisons in their milky sap, the chemicals in this froth may be toxic to vertebrate predators. The frothy fluid gives off a strong smell that serves as the initial warning to potential predators and is similar to that produced by species of ladybirds that are also toxic to predators.

**HABITAT:** Found in rainforest.

**DISTRIBUTION:** From Cooktown in Qld to Northern NSW, as well as north-west WA and NT.

**SIZE:** The adult wingspan is 58 mm.

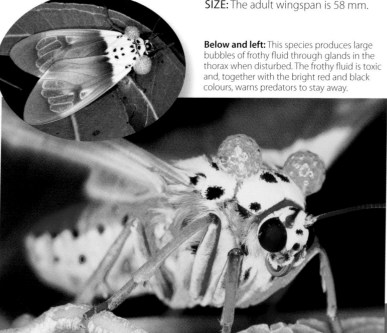

**Below and left:** This species produces large bubbles of frothy fluid through glands in the thorax when disturbed. The frothy fluid is toxic and, together with the bright red and black colours, warns predators to stay away.

# Owlets
## Family: Noctuidae

Owlets are the largest family of moths in the world. They are also called armyworms, cutworms or semi-loopers. The family includes small to very large moths in a fantastic array of colours, shapes and sizes. Many species are drab brown but most species within the family are characterised by a kidney-shaped marking about two-thirds of the way along the forewings. Wingspan varies between 10–170 mm.

Being such a large family, owlets are found in every terrestrial habitat in Australia. Adults are strong fliers and most species are nocturnal, although a few notable exceptions, such as the vine moths, are day-flying. Most adults feed at flowers or suck the juice from fruit, particularly the fruit of rainforest plants. This family also includes overseas species that drink tears or suck the blood of cattle.

The round eggs are usually laid on the leaves of the moth's food plants, either singly or in groups. In some species, the female covers the eggs with scales from her abdomen. Many caterpillars have lost the middle legs of the body, giving them an appearance similar to loopers when they move.

Depending on the species, they may feed openly during the day or shelter by day and feed at night. The caterpillars may feed on leaves, buds, flowers, fruit or seeds of numerous species of food plant. This moth family includes some of the most damaging insect pests in Australia.

More than 1000 species are known from Australia and there are at least 35,000 species worldwide.

**Top:** Some owlets may be confused with the moths of other families because of their striking patterns of black and white with red or yellow. **Right:** Some of the most serious insect pests in Australia belong to this family.

This is one of the most common caterpillars in south-eastern Australia during summer. Although large groups of caterpillars can cause significant damage to their host gum trees, the trees quickly recover.

**DESCRIPTION:** Males and females are very similar to each other. They are dull grey with black lines across the forewings and, despite their abundance during summer, are rarely seen.

**LIFE HISTORY:** Small yellow eggs are laid either singly or in groups on gum leaves. The young caterpillars feed in a group on the surface of the leaf and later move off to feed individually, consuming the leaf tissue between the veins and leaving only a leaf skeleton. They feed throughout summer on a number of gum species. These caterpillars are best known for their covering of stinging hairs; each hair is connected to a venom gland containing histamine, causing a stinging sensation and a raised welt, followed by a persistent itchy rash if touched. Each time the caterpillars shed their skin, they leave the old head capsule from the previous moult attached to the head of the new moult. The caterpillars grow to 25 mm and, when fully fed, pupate in cocoons, which retain the stinging hairs, in sheltered sites. The cocoon also retains the old head capsule from the caterpillar.

**BEHAVIOUR:** They are nocturnal. Adults may be seen flying during summer and autumn.

**HABITAT:** Found in eucalypt forests and suburban areas.

**DISTRIBUTION:** Qld, NSW, ACT, Vic, SA.

**SIZE:** The adult wingspan is about 30 mm.

**Below:** This species has also been called the "hatterpillar", due to the stack of old head capsules which are retained after moulting. **Right:** Groups of Gum Leaf Skeletonisers are a common sight on small gum trees during summer.

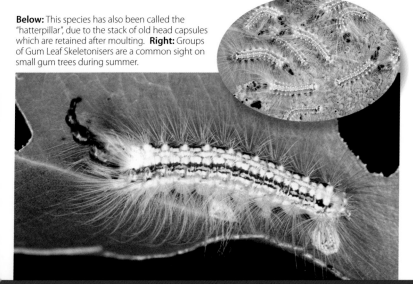

*The Silver Y Moth is also called the Tobacco Looper. A native moth, it has adapted well to feeding on introduced plants such as potato, cabbages, herbs and tobacco.*

**DESCRIPTION:** The forewing has two characteristic silver-gold markings, which may vary slightly in different parts of this moth's range. The sexes look very similar to each other.

**LIFE HISTORY:** The female lays up to 1500 eggs on the underside of the leaves of a range of native and introduced plants, including herbs, *Pelargonium* species, vetch, cabbages and cauliflowers. In some areas they can be a minor pest. The caterpillar grows to 45 mm and is light green with a white line down each side and small white dots all over the body. Caterpillars feed at night and rest underneath leaves by day. Young caterpillars scrape the surface off the underside of leaves, but later chew ragged holes in the foliage. Development takes four to six weeks in summer, and up to nine weeks in winter. When finished feeding, the caterpillar pupates in a silken cocoon among leaves of the food plant or in leaf litter. The caterpillars are found during summer and autumn.

**BEHAVIOUR:** Adults are nocturnal but are most commonly seen resting during the day, sometimes in exposed locations. They are on the wing from November to February.

**HABITAT:** Prefers agricultural and horticultural areas, roadsides and suburban areas.

**DISTRIBUTION:** Occurs over most of Australia.

**SIZE:** The adult wingspan is 30–40 mm.

**Below:** This native species can be a minor pest to introduced crops. The markings on the wings can vary from one locality to the next. **Right:** The caterpillar of this species is often mistaken for a looper caterpillar, as it moves in a very similar fashion.

*This genus includes a number of species that are pests on a wide range of crops, such as tomatoes, cabbages and cotton. The Lily Moth, however, feeds only on lilies but can sometimes be a minor pest.*

DESCRIPTION: Adults sit with the wings held roof-like over the body. Males and females look very similar to each other in colour and pattern. The thorax is covered with thick orange-brown scales and the wings are patterned with red, black and brown on a white background.

LIFE HISTORY: The eggs are laid in a group on the leaves of food plants, which are Swamp Lily, Crinum Lilies, starflowers and the Kaffir Lily. The eggs are covered with scales from the female's abdomen. Young caterpillars feed in groups and skeletonise the leaves, but after the first moult they feed alone, either consuming the whole leaf or boring into the heart of the food plant. The caterpillar is hairless and has many thin, irregular, brownish-black and white stripes down the length, with a thicker dark yellow stripe down each side and another down the back. The rear end is slightly humped, with a large black spot on each side.

BEHAVIOUR: Lily Moths are nocturnal. Very little has been recorded about the behaviour of this species. Adults are most commonly seen sitting on foliage during the day.

HABITAT: Found in rainforest and moist forests where their food plants occur.

DISTRIBUTION: Torres Strait Islands, Qld and NSW as far south as Batemans Bay.

SIZE: The adult wingspan is 45 mm.

*Adult Granny's Cloak Moths are host to the* Dasypodia *mite, which does not appear to have much impact on the moths. The mites probably attach themselves when the moths are hiding in dark places during the day.*

**DESCRIPTION:** Adults have an intricate pattern of dark brown and blue-grey zig-zagging lines across the wings. The colours appear to change slightly, depending on the angle of viewing. The pattern of the forewings continues onto the hindwings, helping with camouflage. The eyespots on the wings are probably used to deter predators. Adults sit with their wings spread out and pressed onto the surface on which they are resting.

**LIFE HISTORY:** Surprisingly little is known of the life history of this species and the caterpillars have not been studied. The food plants are various species of wattles. Adults are eaten by birds and particularly by bats.

**BEHAVIOUR:** This species is nocturnal and often enters houses and other buildings to hide in dark corners during the day. They also roost in caves and stormwater drains, sometimes in large numbers. When roosting together, they align their bodies in the same direction, which seems to help with camouflage. Adults often come to lights at night. They may undertake short migrations when winds are strong and have been found on islands up to 80 km off the Australian coast.

**HABITAT:** Found in rainforest and related areas.

**DISTRIBUTION:** From Atherton Tablelands in Qld to central NSW. Also found in NT.

**SIZE:** Both the male and female wingspan is 75 mm.

# Bogong Moth *Agrotis infusa*

*This species is one of the most well-known moths in Australia. Millions of moths migrate together over thousands of kilometres across south-eastern Australia every year to shelter in the cool caves of the Snowy Mountains*

**DESCRIPTION:** Adults are dull grey-brown with two distinctive spots on each forewing. Males and females are very similar.

**LIFE HISTORY:** Eggs are laid on leaves of herbaceous plants, including weeds and pasture crops, such as capeweed, medicago and saltbushes. The green or brownish caterpillars are known as cutworms. During the day they shelter in the soil and emerge at night to feed. They pupate in the soil and adults appear in winter. By late spring, adults migrate to the Australian Alps to shelter from the heat of summer. At the end of February, the moths begin to migrate back to the breeding grounds to lay eggs. Adults feed on flowers as well as the honeydew produced by lerp insects.

**BEHAVIOUR:** Adults are active at night and are frequently attracted to lights. When sheltering in caves and among rocky outcrops, they select moist crevices away from the wind, but if large numbers are present they may sit on the open rock faces. Most individuals remain immobile for the entire period, but some may emerge after dusk to fly around the mountaintops.

**HABITAT:** They exist in a range of habitats, particularly open plains, pasture and other croplands.

**DISTRIBUTION:** Qld, NSW, Vic.

**SIZE:** Male wingspan is 42 mm; female wingspan is 45 mm.

# Glossary

**ABDOMEN** The last or final section of the body of an invertebrate. In butterflies and moths it is the last of the three main subdivisions (following head and thorax).

**ANTENNA (PLURAL ANTENNAE)** Paired appendages on the heads of insects and some other invertebrates, used for sensing chemicals, windspeed and other features.

**CAMOUFLAGE** A strategy whereby animals disguise themselves to blend in with the background by modifying their colour, pattern or shape.

**COCOON** The silken, protective covering spun by moth caterpillars just before pupating within it.

**DORSAL HORN** A long, stiff spike at the end of the abdomen of hawk moth caterpillars.

**ECHOLOCATION** Method used by animals such as bats and dolphins to locate objects by determining (by radar or sonar) time for an echo to return and direction from which it returns.

**EXOSKELETON** The tough outer covering of insects, literally an external skeleton.

**EYESPOT** A coloured spot on the wing of butterflies or moths, designed to look like eyes to frighten potential predators.

**FAMILY** A group of closely related genera.

**FLANGE** A rim, ridge or flap that sticks out from the body of some animals.

**FRASS** The faeces, or droppings, of insects.

**GENUS (PLURAL GENERA)** A grouping of closely related species.

**HEAD CAPSULE** The hard, rounded head of a caterpillar, containing the eyes and the mouthparts.

**HILLTOPPING** A strategy whereby male butterflies collect at the tops of hills to set up territories and wait for passing females.

**LARVA (PLURAL LARVAE)** The immature stage of an insect that undergoes metamorphosis (pupates) into an adult. In butterflies and moths it is called a caterpillar.

**LEPIDOPTERA** An order of insects that comprises butterflies and moths.

**MANDIBLES** The major components of an insect's mouthparts. They are usually designed for chewing but may be modified for other purposes.

**METAMORPHOSIS** A process by which an immature insect (e.g. a caterpillar) transforms into an adult (e.g. a butterfly), sometimes inside a cocoon. The larval body is broken down and the new adult insect is built in its place.

**MIGRATION** A large scale movement of animals in one general direction.

**MIMICRY** A process whereby one species resembles another species occurring in the same area to its own advantage. The mimicking species may also resemble a non-living object, such as a bird dropping.

**MISTLETOE** A group of plants that attach themselves to the branch of a tree and usually grow high up in the canopy.

**MOULT** The process by which insects, arachnids and crustaceans shed their skin to increase their body size as they grow.

**MUTUALISM** An interaction between two different species in which both species benefit.

**NOCTURNAL** Active at night.

**OCELLI (SINGULAR OCELLUS)** Simple, light-sensitive organs on the head of insects, in addition to the normal eyes.

**OMMATIDIUM** A single component of the compound eyes of insects.

**ORDER** A group of closely related families of animals.

**OSMETERIUM** A soft, forked, organ found behind the head of caterpillars of the family Papilionidae (swallowtails) that is able to be everted (turned inside out). It is usually strong smelling and is used for defence.

**OVERWINTER** Similar to hibernation, where insects survive the winter months with little or no activity.

**PARASITE** A plant or animal completely dependent on the body of another plant or animal for its food, sometimes killing the host when fully fed.

**PHEROMONES** A chemical smell given off by one animal that influences the behaviour of other animals of the same species, usually used by females to attract males for mating.

**PROBOSCIS** A tubular organ in insects, comprised of fused mouthparts used for sucking up liquid food.

**PROLEGS** The fleshy legs of caterpillars, which may extend down the length of the body. They are different to the three pairs of true legs directly behind the head.

**PTERINE PIGMENTS** Special pigments found in the bodies of butterflies in the family Pieridae, which give them their white and yellow background colours.

**PUPA (PLURAL PUPAE)** The non-feeding stage of metamorphosing insects between the larva and the adult.

**PUPATE** The act of becoming a pupa.

**REFLEX BLEEDING** A defensive strategy employed by some insects (and other animals) whereby they deliberately leak their toxic blood through special openings in the body.

**SCOLI** An outgrowth from the body wall of a caterpillar, often branched or bearing hairs.

**SEX SCALES** Specially designed scales on the body or wings of a butterfly or moth that are impregnated with pheromones and used to attract a mate.

**SPECIES** A genetically distinct group of animals that can breed together to produce fertile young but are unable to interbreed successfully with other, similar animals. Each species has a two word scientific name e.g. *Danaus plexippus* (the Wanderer Butterfly).

**SPIRACLE** The external opening of the trachea, the breathing system of insects and other invertebrates.

**STARTLE DISPLAY** An alarm response in many animal species, particularly insects. Eyespots or warning colours are suddenly

displayed in response to disturbance, in an effort to deter predators.

**SUBSPECIES** A distinct population within a species, which is notably different to other populations within the same species. Different subspecies are able to interbreed.

**TERRESTRIAL** Living on land.

**THANATOSIS** Feigning death. Many insects pretend to be dead when threatened.

**THORAX** The middle section of an insect, between the head and abdomen. It usually bears three pairs of legs and two pairs of wings.

**TORNUS** The lowest point on the hindwing of a butterfly or moth when the wing is held straight out from the body.

**TRACHEA** Respiratory tubes stretching from the outer spiracles to the internal organs of insects and other invertebrates.

**TUBERCLE** A small, round outgrowth of the body of a caterpillar.

**ULTRAVIOLET LIGHT** Light that is above the range of wavelengths visible to humans. It can be seen only with special equipment.

**VERTEBRATES** Animals with backbones.

# Index

# Links & Further Reading

## Books

Braby M.F. *Butterflies of Australia: Their Identification, Biology and Distribution (two volumes)*, CSIRO Publishing, Melbourne, 2000

Common I.F.B. & Waterhouse, D.F. *Butterflies of Australia (revised edition)*, Angus & Robertson Publishers, Sydney, 1981

Common I.F.B. *Australian Moths*, The Jacaranda Press, Brisbane, 1963

Common I.F.B. *Moths of Australia,* Melbourne University Press, Melbourne, 1990

Coupar P. & Coupar M. *Flying Colours: Common Caterpillars, Butterflies and Moths of South-Eastern Australia,* New South Wales University Press, 1992

McCubbin C. *Australian Butterflies,* Thomas Nelson Ltd, Melbourne, 1971

McCubbin C. *How to Breed Butterflies,* The Friends of the Zoo and The Zoological Board of Victoria, Melbourne, 1985

### Field Guides
#### National
Braby M.F. *The Complete Field Guide to Butterflies of Australia*, CSIRO Publishing, Melbourne, 2004

Zborowski P. & Edwards T. *A Guide to Australian Moths,* CSIRO Publishing, Melbourne, 2007

#### Queensland
Ryan M. (Ed.) *Wildlife of Greater Brisbane,* Queensland Museum, Brisbane, 1995

Ryan et al, *Wildlife of Tropical North Queensland,* Queensland Museum, Brisbane, 2000

#### South Australia
Fisher R.H. *Butterflies of South Australia,* South Australian Government, Adelaide, 1978

McQuillan P.B. & Forrest J.A.A. *Guide to Common Moths of the Adelaide Region,* South Australian Museum, Adelaide, 1985

#### Victoria
Birch B. and others. *Melbourne's Wildlife: A Guide to the Fauna of Greater Melbourne*, Museum Victoria and CSIRO Publishing, Melbourne, 2006

## Websites

### Australian Butterflies & Moths

www.csiro.au/org/EntomologyResources.html

www.ento.csiro.au/gallery/moths

www.jcu.edu.au/discovernature/
butterfliescommon/index.htm

www.environment.gov.au/biodiversity/
threatened/publications/action/butterfly/pubs/
butterflies.pdf

www.usyd.edu.au/museums/larvae/

### Australian Museums

Australian Museum **www.amonline.net.au**

Qld — **www.qm.ld.gov.au**

WA — **www.museum.wa.gov.au**

SA — **www.samuseum.sa.gov.au**

Vic — **www.museumvictoria.com.au**

Tas — **www.tmag.tas.gov.au**

NT — **www.nt.gov.au**

### Regional Sites

New South Wales **www.faunanet.gov.au**

Published by Steve Parish Publishing Pty Ltd
PO Box 1058, Archerfield, Qld 4108 Australia

**www.steveparish.com.au**

© Steve Parish Publishing

ISBN 978174193406 9

First published 2008

Text and photography: Patrick Honan

Front cover image: Orange Lacewings (*Cethosia penthesilea*) mating.

Title page main image: Wanderer caterpillar
Inset, from top to bottom: Wanderer pupa;
Cairns Birdwing Butterfly (male).

Design: Gill Stack, SPP
Editing: Robyn Dunsford; Michele Perry, Helen Anderson & Jason Negus, SPP;
Production: Tina Brewster, SPP

Prepress by Colour Chiefs Digital Imaging, Brisbane, Australia
Printed in Singapore by Imago

**Produced in Australia at the Steve Parish Publishing Studios**